Leland Lewis Duncan

The Parish Church of Saint Mary in Lewisham, Kent

Its Building and Rebuilding

Leland Lewis Duncan

The Parish Church of Saint Mary in Lewisham, Kent
Its Building and Rebuilding

ISBN/EAN: 9783337336585

Printed in Europe, USA, Canada, Australia, Japan

Cover: Foto ©Lupo / pixelio.de

More available books at **www.hansebooks.com**

The Parish Church

of

Saint Mary, Lewisham,

Kent,

Its Building and Rebuilding;

with some account of the

Vicars and Curates of Lewisham.

By

Leland L. Duncan, F.S.A.

Honorary Secretary of the Lewisham Antiquarian Society.

Printed by
Charles North at Blackheath, in the Parish of Lewisham.
1892.

✠

To my Mother, Caroline Ellen Duncan,
this story of the House
wherein we sometime walked together
is reverently dedicated.

✠

.

Preface.

THIS short history of the Parish Church of St. Mary, Lewisham, is an expansion of a paper prepared for the seventh annual meeting of the Lewisham Antiquarian Society, and which the members very kindly expressed a desire to possess in print. In acceding to the request I have taken the opportunity of adding certain details which would have been tedious on that occasion, but which are worthy of record—such as the notes on lights and images in mediæval times, the chantries, the inventories of church goods in 1552 and 1892, the vicarage-house, &c., &c.; and, lastly, some account of the vicars and curates of Lewisham, all of which I hope will prove of interest to parishioners.

In order that the pages should not be burdened with references—which, although desirable from a critical point of view, are apt to be troublesome to the reader—I subjoin here a list of authorities for the facts recorded:—

Notices of lights, images, gifts of ornaments, &c., and bequests to the building of the tower, to the church gilds, &c.—*Wills proved in the Consistory Court of Rochester and in the Prerogative Court of Canterbury.* These I have gone through carefully and have extracted all bequests to the church that were of interest.

Matters relating to the rebuilding of the church—*The Minute-book of the Trustees* (now in the vestry safe).

Monumental inscriptions in the old church—*Thorpe's " Registrum Roffense."* (These inscriptions were reprinted by the society in 1889, together with those in the churchyard and present church, and I have, consequently, not reproduced them in full here.)

The Papal Bull, printed on page 2—*Kimbell's* "*Charities of Greenwich.*"

The chantry certificate—*Public Record Office, Chantry Certificates, Nos. 28 and 29.*

The Parochial Registers have yielded a few interesting notes as to the interments within the building. So much of the registers from 1558 to 1750 as now exists was printed in 1891.

I am also beholden to a very useful article in the "*Messager des Sciences Historiques de Belgique*" for 1842, by the Baron JULES DE SAINT-GENOIS, on the documents in the archives of Flanders relating to England, which appears to have escaped the notice of our local historians. Many of the charters quoted by him have reference to Lewisham, and among the witnesses are two early vicars of the parish whose names have not hitherto been recorded. Dr. DRAKE'S new edition of *Hasted's* "*Hundred of Blackheath*" has also given me the name of another vicar in the reign of Henry V—Richard Chapman; and for the general history of the parish I cannot do better than refer the reader to that work, which is full of detail of inestimable value to the genealogist.

The inventory of church goods, 1552, is (by permission) taken from Vol. IX, "*Archæologia Cantiana*," and the indenture at the head of the same has been communicated to me by my friend Mr. ARTHUR BARRON.

I desire likewise to express my best thanks to all those who have given me information on the various points here dealt with. Especially am I indebted to the Right Rev. the Lord Bishop of LICHFIELD for many notes as to the changes during his vicariate; to the present vicar, the Rev. SAMUEL BICKERSTETH, and to the churchwardens, Messrs. T. A. WARRINGTON and R. HARDY SMITH, who have placed at my disposal all the records now in their custody.

In the following pages I have principally confined myself to matters relating to the fabric and ornaments of the church, but I may just refer here to the prominent part played by the building in the life of the people, of which there are many glimpses from time to time in the public records. There is, for instance, the scene, so tersely described in *The Assize Rolls*, 1254, in the reign of Henry the Third, when Geoffrey le Bidelede and Margery David, having beaten to death Agnes the daughter of one Roger le Biche, were brought before the court of the Prior of Lewisham, as representing the lord of the manor, and imprisoned pending trial. Margery, however, effected her escape from the Prior's prison and fled to the parish church, and afterwards, before William Scot the bailiff, abjured the realm (*vide* DRAKE's Hasted, p. 281).

Such incidents, perhaps, more properly belong to the general history of the parish than to that of the fabric of the church, and with others may possibly, on a future occasion, form the subject of a paper dealing with the customs of the manor and the life of the villagers.

If those into whose hands this book may fall can add anything, however seemingly trivial, to that which I have here recorded, or should they possess drawings or plans, either of the church or any portion of the parish, they will, by communicating with me, not only be doing me a kindness, but they will at the same time be helping forward the object for which our local society exists.

" *Rosslair*,"　　　　　　　　　　　　　　　LELAND L. DUNCAN.
　Lewisham, 1892.

Contents.

...

Illustrations.

The
Parish Church of St. Mary, Lewisham.

I.

Sketch of the History of the Manor and Advowson.

Although it does not come within the scope of an account of Lewisham Parish Church to enter fully into the history of the Manor, yet the civil history of the place is so bound up with the ecclesiastical that it is well nigh impossible to touch one without—at least, to some extent—entering on the other. A brief record therefore, firstly, of the various hands through which the manor has passed, and the names of those who from time to time have had the right of presentation to the vicarage, will not, it is hoped, be considered out of place here.

It is a long story, that of "the place which the rustics from ancient custom "have called Lievesham," as King Edgar describes it in his charter. It takes us back to the days of Alfred the Great, whose youngest daughter, Ethelswitha, received as an inheritance the district of Lewisham, with its appendages of Greenwich and Woolwich. She married Baldwin, Count of Flanders, and in 918, by deed, conveyed her property to the Abbey of St. Peter in Ghent, and the grant was confirmed by subsequent kings. Whether a church existed here in those early times it is not possible to say. The probability is that, soon after the grant, the monks of Ghent would have sent over some official to manage the property for them and look after their rents and dues, and that a building for Divine worship would have been erected, if one did not then already exist. There is, it is true, no mention of a church in the Doomsday account of Lewisham; but, as the Commissioners were not specially authorized to enquire under that head, it cannot be taken as a proof that a church did not exist at the date of the Survey, indeed, in the confirmatory charter of King Edgar in 964, before quoted, the words "with their churches, churchyards," &c., are included.

The church was appropriated in the reign of Henry II by the Bishop of Rochester to the Abbey of St. Peter at Ghent, the abbey undertaking to present a clerk who should serve in the church as vicar.

The Abbot of Ghent evidently had considerable difficulty in retaining his hold on the property, and we find that almost every king at some time during his reign was constrained to grant a confirmatory charter upholding the monastery in its possessions. Pope Eugenius III and Pope Alexander III both issued Bulls, addressed to the Archbishop of Canterbury and the Bishop of Rochester, taking Lewisham and Greenwich under the protection of the Holy See. A further Bull of Pope Alexander III, circa 1170, to the Abbot of Ghent may be quoted as of local interest :—

" Alexander, Bishop, servant of the servants of God, to his beloved children,
" the abbot and brethren of St. Peter of Gant, safety and apostolic benediction.
" To religious places, by how much the more devoutly God Almighty is in them
" worshipped and adored, by so much the more willingly we ought to impart our
" patronage of apostolic defence, and cherish them with readier consideration.
" Induced by this consideration, and following the footsteps of the happy memory
" of our father and predecessor, Pope Eugenius, we have taken Lewisham and
" Greenwich, with their churches and appendages, and other possessions reasonably
" belonging to you, under our protection, and that of the happy Peter; and we
" have strengthened it by the patronage of this our present writing, decreeing
" that it is by no means lawful for any man to infringe this page of our protection,
" or in any way to oppose it ; and if any one shall presume to attempt it, let him
" know that he will incur the displeasure of the Omnipotent God, and of Peter
" and Paul, his happy apostles.   Given at Avigne, 2ᵈ May."

Notwithstanding all these precautions, manors which were in the hands of foreign houses, like that at Ghent, were often seized by the Crown when at war with France, in order to prevent money leaving this country for the support of the King's enemies—the property being returned to the original holders on peace being declared. We find that Lewisham was resumed in this way in the reigns of Edward III and Richard II, and the King presented to the benefice during the time it was in his hands.

There is no doubt that the possession by foreign abbeys of property in this country was, and became more and more, unpopular, and at length, in the reign of Henry V, the Commons presented a petition to the King for the suppression of the Alien Priories, as they were called. In 1414, a statute declared the whole of these properties seized and vested in the Crown, and in the following year, in spite of the protests of the Abbot of Ghent, the King settled the manor of Lewisham, with the advowson, etc., on his newly-founded Priory at Shene in Surrey.

It continued in the possession of Shene Priory until 1531, when Henry VIII

—after failing to oust the Prior on a legal quibble—obtained the manor of Lewis-ham in exchange, in order to enlarge his Greenwich property.

In 1547 Edward VI granted the manor, etc, to his uncle, Thomas, Lord Seymour of Sudeley, but on the attainder of the latter in 1549 Lewisham came again into the King's hands, and so remained until the reign of James the First, for although it was granted away, or leased, more than once, yet from one cause or another it returned to the Crown.

In 1624 James I granted the manor to John, Earl of Holderness, who in 1600 had been instrumental in detecting the plot of Earl Gowry against the King's life. The Earl died without male heir, and the property went to his brother, Sir George Ramsay, whose son, John Ramsay of Winlaton in Durham, sold the manor with the advowson, etc., to Reynold Graham of Humington in Yorkshire, a citizen and draper of London.

Mr. Graham married Susanna, daughter of Sir William Washington of Paking-ton, and enjoys the distinction of being the only Lord of the Manor who is buried in the Parish Church. He had no children, and by deed dated 30th May, 1673, he conveyed the manor and advowson to his nephew, George Legge, afterwards Baron Dartmouth, in whose family it has remained to the present time.

We may, therefore, summarize the ownership of Lewisham as follows :—

The Abbey of St. Peter at Ghent ...	918 to 1414
The Priory of Shene	1414 to 1531
The Crown, etc.	1531 to 1624
The Ramsays	1624 to 1640
Raynold Graham	1640 to 1673
The Legges	1673 to the present.

II

Dedication of the Church.

The Parish Church of Lewisham is dedicated to the Blessed Virgin Mary. This is without doubt the original dedication. In 1229 Pope Gregory decided that certain tithes in this parish should belong to the Abbey of Bermondsey, which house should pay to the Abbot of Ghent two wax candles, of $1\frac{1}{2}$ lbs., in the chapel of the Blessed Mary at Lewisham, on the Vigil of the Feast of the Nativity of the Virgin (8th September)—probably a parochial festival day. Another day of note in the parish was the Feast of the Purification (2nd February), as we learn from an agreement made in 1431 between Dr. William Frome, the Vicar, and the Prior and Convent of Shene, by which the Vicar gave up his right to certain tithes, receiving instead half the wax offered in the church on that day—a profitable arrangement no doubt in 1431, but scarcely so at the present day. In further proof of the dedication it may be worth while to note that in mediæval times persons living here invariably desire that they should be buried " in the church or churchyard of Our " Lady in Lewisham."

III.

The Ancient Nave.

At the present time (1892) the church consists of a western tower, the base of which is of late fifteenth century architecture, the topmost storey having been added in 1774 ; a nave built in 1774-77 on the site of an older one ; and a chancel, with short north and south transepts, erected in 1881. I propose firstly to trace the history of the old church, together with that of the tower, then to touch upon the rebuilding of 1774, and finally on the remodelling of 1882.

We have, unfortunately, no plans or drawings of the original church except a small sketch in Drake's History from the Beresford Hope collection, from which, together with a photograph of the base of the tower, the accompanying illustration is derived ; but we learn from a description published by J. C. Barrow in 1790 that the entrance was by a large porch, descending one step, and into the church two steps more ; thus the floor was level with the vaults under the present church. The church had a double roof (that is, consisted of a nave and aisle, each with a separate roof), the east end supported by a large central pillar, from which sprang the arches of the roof ; the ceiling was painted, rudely representing clouds, stars, etc. The floor was paved with small square tiles. In the body of the church were four rows of pews, the two middle rows joined, the side rows being separated by an aisle quite round the church. The pulpit and reading desk were placed against the north wall.

Such is the description given us by one who had seen the old building before its destruction, and there are many small village churches which will help us to picture pretty correctly what St. Mary's was like in the middle of the last century.

The chief entrance before 1774, as now, was by a large porch on the south side of the church. There are no details concerning the porch in the wills of

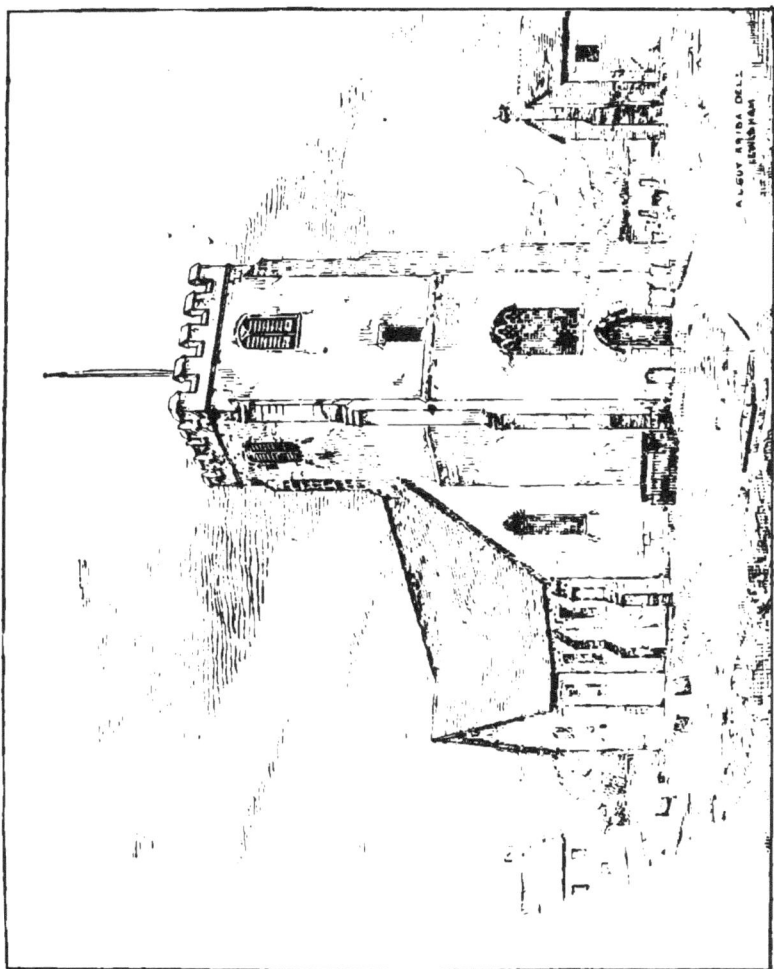

Lewisham Church, 1770.

parishioners, but it is mentioned several times in the registers. Thus in 1560 we are told that "Sr Peter Marton, parson of Clomnynge, who was murthered " in the little lane from Southend to Bromley, was buried at the porch door." In 1738 Lucretia, wife of Abraham Battersby, was buried "next ye Porch'd door."

Of the appearance of this side of the church in 1656 we have a glimpse in the will of the Rev. Abraham Colfe. In the arrangement for his burial he says : " I desire my executors to see my body buried in a decent and Christian manner, " in the churchyard of Lewisham, close to the wall under the little South window " above the door Eastward that goeth out of the churchyard into the Parish " Chancel . . . . and my will is that a Free stone of about one Foot broad " and square every way and Three Foote long shall be set deep and upright in the " ground over my grave, to uphold a strong thick Plank of Oak, which shall be " put there all along close by the wall, between the two Buttresses, for People to sit " upon when they resort to the Public Church Meetings." This kindly thoughtfulness for his parishioners, many of whom would in those days have had to plod a considerable distance to church, was doubtless fully appreciated.

The body of the church was divided into two aisles, called respectively the men's aisle and the women's aisle, as appears from entries in the burial register :—

1740, March 9.   Mr. John Bellew buried in ye women's Oyle.

1745, July 10.   Capt. Thos. Trevor in ye middle of ye women's Isle.

1747, Nov. 24.   Mr. John Marks in the women's Isle.

1748, Aug. 1.   Thomas Maidstone, Esq., in ye men's Isle.

1755, Aug. 5.   Mrs. Holiman in the men's Isle close to the side of Mr. Hide's Pew.

1756, June 18.   Mrs. Sarah Small in the men's Isle.

1759, Jan. 5.   Mr. John Small from Deptford in the men's isle opposite the pew where the bread is given.

It would seem from these and similar entries that the old custom of dividing the sexes was kept up here until quite late in the 18th century, or it may be only the recollection of the once existing use.

Another burial worth noting is that of Mrs. Jane Valentine in 1741, who was " buried in the church by the Pillar." This last is evidently the central supporting column noticed by Barrow, and of which we shall hear more when we come to the rebuilding of the nave.

In 1725 Mrs. Ann Swinburn from Holbourn was buried "in the Oyle opposite " against the Deske," for which Dr. Stanhope, in his diary of receipts, notes that he received three guineas.

In the northern aisle was a mural monument to Mr. John Pery and his family, 1732; and in the south aisle was another to Thomas Dyer, Esq., and his wife, 1748.

In the south aisle was a gallery supported by wooden columns. I have not been able to trace its first erection, unless it was put up by Mr. Colfe. In his will,

dated 1656, he arranges for the teaching of thirty poor boys, and desires that "the
" Schoolmaster shall, every Lord's day, both forenoon and afternoon, in Time of
" Health, come duly to the public church of Lewisham, and set in the fore front of
" the Gallery, and carefully look to the Free scholars appointed to come to Church
" Daily, and to set in the Gallery built for that purpose, near unto him, and to
" behave themselves reverently there all the Time of Divine service and sermon,
" and "—he adds—"he may do well to write down Notes of the Sermons"! In
the Burial Register for 1753 is the entry, "Mrs. Joanna Rigby from Greenwich,
" in the south aisle at the foot of the gallery stairs."

IV.

The Chancels.

There were two chancels in the old building—one at the east end of each of
the aisles, the northern being the high chancel. Thorpe states that in the principal
chancel there was, on the north side, a stone coffin cased over with board, which
formed a seat in two pews near the rails of the Communion Table. When the
old church was pulled down there was a stone coffin in this position, but level
with the floor, with a stone lid, which was taken up and examined. The skeleton
was nearly entire, and the hair perfect. It was buried under the present vaults.
At the time, this was taken to have been the coffin of one of the priors of the
monastery which formerly existed in this parish at Rushy Green. It was more
probably the burial place of John Glyn, Vicar, who died in 1568, and who desired
in his will to be buried "in the north side of the high chauncell at Lewsham in a
" tomb of marble stone."

On the floor of the chancel was a gravestone to Mrs. Susanna Grahme, second
daughter of Sir William Washington, and wife of Reginald Grahme, Esq., once
Lord of the Manor. She died in 1698. Her sister, Elizabeth, married William
Legge, father of the first Baron Dartmouth, to whom this manor was conveyed by
Mr. Grahme, as before related. There were also gravestones to Mary Griffith, 1647 ;
Anne, daughter of Sir William Wylde, 1668, and Frances Wylde, another daughter
of the same, 1666—victims, probably, of the great plague. On the south side of
the altar was another stone to William Rutland, 1696. Within the altar rails was
buried Dr. Stanhope, Dean of Canterbury and Vicar here, who died in 1727; also
George, son of William Hatteclyff (a member of the family which gave Lewisham
the Almshouses at Catford), who died in 1514, and to whom was an effigy in brass,

Brass of GEORGE HATTECLYFF, 1514, formerly in St. Mary's Church, Lewisham.
The inscription is now affixed to the North Wall: the figure, lost some years since,
is copied from an engraving in THORPE's "*Custumale Roffense.*"

with his coat of arms. The figure is lost, but the inscription is fixed in the north wall of the present church :

> HIC IACET GEORGIUS FILIUS ET HERES WILLMI HATTECLYFF ARMIG'I
> QUŌDAM THESAURAM TERRE DÑI REGIS HIBERNIE AC VNIS CL'ICORUM
> COMPOTI HOSPICIJ REGS QUI QUIDĒ GEORGIUS OBIJT P'MO DIE MĒSIS
> AUGUSTI ANNO DÑI MILLMO QUINGENTESIMO DECIMO QUARTO.

The accompanying representation of the brass, for which I am indebted to Mr. H. Richardson, is from a sketch in Thorpe's *Custumale Roffense*, so far as the figure is concerned, and the inscription is from a rubbing of the original.

On the north wall were monuments to Mrs. Margaret Colfe, wife of Abraham Colfe, Vicar, 1643 ; to Thomas Jones, Esq., Common Serjeant of the City of London, 1625 ; to Dr. Stanhope, Vicar, 1727, and another to Olivia Cotton, his first wife, 1707.

Another interesting memorial which, if it were ever erected, soon disappeared, was that to the Stoddards, a leading family at Mottingham, in the adjoining parish of Eltham. Fortunately, Sir Nicholas Stoddard, in his will proved in 1636, expressed pretty fully his wishes in this respect—" I will to be buried in Lewsham " in the parrish church and a stone shall be layd upon my wife and myself, with " our pictures of brasse with the inscriptions what wee were, and whence wee were, " what yeare we died and of what age."

The chancel at the eastern end of the south aisle was dedicated to the Holy Trinity. The first mention I find of it is in 1463, when Steven Levendale left iij iiijᵈ thereto. In 1471 William Sprigg, who started the rebuilding of the tower, desired that his tenements in the occupation of John Crokker and John Goldyng should be sold, and the proceeds expended in finding a priest to celebrate in the church of Lewisham, at the altar of the Holy Trinity, for the souls of himself, his father and mother, and his friends. In 1498 Robert Cheseman, the elder, gentleman, gave directions that he was to be interred within the chapel of the Trinity within the parish church of Lewisham, before the image of Saint John Baptist nigh unto the wall there. His widow, Johan Cheseman, in her will dated 2nd April, 1527, desired to be buried "in the Trinite chauncell off the churche off " oure lady off Levesham nygh the plasse wher as the body of Robᵗ Cheseman, " my husband, lyethe bured," showing that his wish was fulfilled. In 1511 John Robyns directed that he was to be buried in the " Trynitie chapell."

Before this part of the old church was taken down in 1774, there were gravestones in the south chancel to Mr. Thomas Curteis, 1728 ; John Peter, gent, 1684 ; and John Dyer, gent, 1713. On the south wall were monuments to Mrs. Mary Symes, 1702 ; Richard Symes, 1728 ; and Mrs. Elizabeth Dyer, 1708.

It was in the south chancel that the two chantries in this church were founded. Particulars regarding these will be found under a separate heading. When the chantries were abolished in 1547, and the altar of the Trinity taken away, the proprietary right to this chancel seems to have passed to the Vicar—as all the persons above mentioned (and others who were buried therein) are expressly stated in the Register to be buried "in the Vicar's chancel," as distinguished from "the chancel." Dr. Stanhope, in his account book, has these entries—"August 5th, 1700, for Boards and work for seats in the Vicar's chancel, " repaired and made at my charge, £3," and "April, 1727, P^d Corbet the Carpenter " for repairing the Pew late of Mrs. Lucas in the Vicar's chancel, £1 7s. od.," and on 3rd August, 1694, the burial of Mr. William Stodard "in my chancell" is noted.

In addition to the foregoing there was a chapel in the church dedicated to the Blessed Virgin. This was begun about 1500, as appears by the will of Richard Howcheson, who left 3s. 4d. "to the byldying of o^r lady chapell w^t in " the church;" and in this chapel several persons desired in their wills that they were to be buried. In the sketch of the old church there will be seen a small out-building on the north side of the nave. This I take to be the chapel referred to, and its subsequent use as a vestry would account for the absence of any record by Thorpe of monumental inscriptions in that part of the building.

In 1502 Thomas Owterede of Lewisham, tanner, desired his house in Essex to be sold, one half to go to his wife Agnes for the bringing up of his children, and "the other halfe to the church of Lewisham to make the Rode Lofte of the seyde church." The loft thus erected, over which stood the great crucifix, would doubtless have been taken down about 1560, but I have not come across any further details regarding it.

Before leaving this portion of the old church it may be worth while to add a few words on the probable style in which it was built. These must of necessity be brief. When the apse was taken down in 1882 it was found that the walls were composed to some extent of material from the mediæval church, and any pieces of stone which were at all worked were placed on one side. Some were used in repairing the tower arch, and the others are now preserved in the vaults. By the kindness of Mr. Albert Guy I am able to give a drawing of these. They comprise a portion of what was presumably the east window of one of the chancels, of late Perpendicular work but of a very good type, and a portion of a jamb and pier, apparently of the same period; all part, no doubt, of the great "reparacion" carried out when the tower was new built. An older piece of work, a lancet window of Early English type, appears in the sketch of the old church in the western wall to the north of the tower.

Parish Church of S. Mary

Lewisham, Kent

Remains of East Window of Chancel

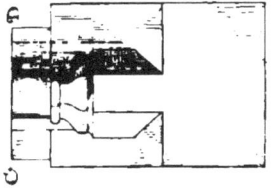

Internal Elevation of Buttress

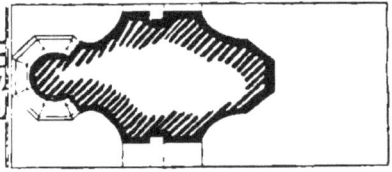

Plan of CD

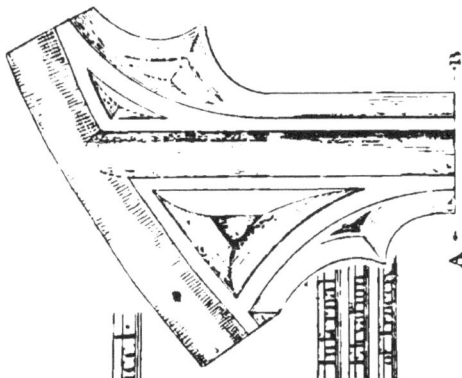

Plan of AB

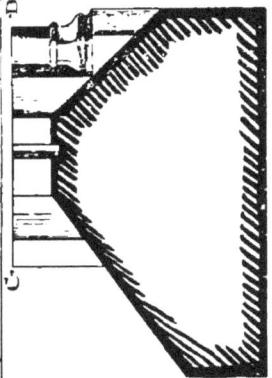

Section of Buttress

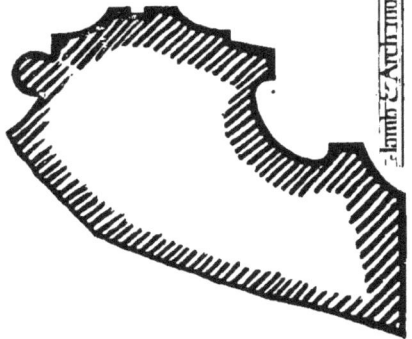

Jamb & Archmould

V.

The Tower.

From the wills of various parishioners we gather that the tower, which stands at the west end of the church, was erected between 1471 and 1512. The originator of the plan seems to have been one William Sprigg, who in 1471 desired that his tenements with their appurtenances situated in East Greenwich should be sold, and the money "disposed toward the new building of the bell tower in the churchyard "of Lewesham."

From that date the contributions flowed in from parishioners of every class, from the five marcs of Richard Walker to the twelve pence of John Kyngston, or those who had no money left a few bushels of corn "to the new making" or reparation of the steeple, until in 1512 William Batt left 26/8 to making the "vice," or stairway. In 1498 Robert Cheseman desired his executors to "glaze "the grete new wyndowe in the belfraye with the picture of the passion of our Lord." Of this, however, if the work was carried out, nothing remains, the glass in the said window, at the present day, being modern.

The following is a list, compiled from wills, of bequests to the building of the tower :—

1473. Cecily, wife of John Lamkyn of Perystrete, vj° viij^d to the making of the
1473. Thomas Edwards iij° iiij^d to the makyng of the stepyll.   [new steeple.
1473. Christian Sprigg, widow, x marcs to the workmanship of the chyrche
1473. William Scott iij° iiij^d to the stepill werks.   [stepyl.
1474. John Crokker, husbandman, vj° viij^d for three years to the fabric of the
1475. Roger Dene iij° to the fabric of the campanile.   [campanile.
1476. John Gossip, smyth, iij° iiij^d to the new wurk of y° new stepille.
1476. John Gwyn vj° viij^d to the work of the new campanile.
1476. Walter Newman xiv° to the new making of the stepill.
1478. Thomas Broke xl^d to the building of the bell tower.   [at Lewisham.
1479. Bernard Cavill of Chislehurst xiij° iiij^d to the building of the bell-tower
1483. John Newman, husbandman, xl^d to the new makyng of the stepyll.
1483. Symon Bate x° to the building of the new bell tower.
1483. John Almayne, xij^d to the operacyons of the new stepyll.   [bell tower.
1484. Roger or Richard Combe ix bushels of corn to the building of the new
1485. Symon Bate, husbandman, x° to the building of the new bell tower.
1486. John Broke xx^d to the reparacion of y° nu stepill.
*1487. John Kyngston xij^d to y° bylding of the nu stepill.
1491. John Johnsone xij^d to the building of the bell tower.   [Leuysham.
1492. Thomas Bedell of Brumlegth, yoman, v° to the makyng of the stepill of
1494. William Feyrewyn xiij° iiij^d to the makyng of the new stepill.
1494. Rychard Walker v marcs to the reparacion and making of the steple.
1498. Robert Cheseman xiij° iiij^d to the reparacion of the stepyll.
1512. William Batt xxvj° viij^d to making the vice of the tower.

---

* John Kyngston also left half his house and garden after the death of his wife Alis to go to
    "y° bildyng of y° stepill in Lewysham."

The tower, as originally built, consisted of two stages, divided into three storeys. The uppermost storey—where the bells were hung, and which is now used as the ringing-room—had four two-light windows, one on each side of the tower ; that on the west only is now open, those on the north and south being closed, and that on the east now looking into the church. The room below this was the original ringing-chamber—it has one small square-headed window on the west side. The lower part of the tower, which has an internal measurement of 11ft. 7in. from north to south, and 14ft. from east to west, then, as now, was open to the church. It has a three-light window on the western side, "the grete new wyndowe" mentioned by Robert Cheseman in 1498, and below it is a doorway with continuous mouldings of the usual Perpendicular character. The tower opens to the church by a lofty archway, having interior shafts with capitals and outer continuous mouldings. The full height of the arch cannot now be seen, as the floor of the church is some ten feet above the old level ; but it is a very fair specimen of the work of the latter part of the 15th century. At the south-east corner of the tower is a spiral staircase —the "vice"—in part the gift of William Batt in 1512. The walls are built of flint, rubble and Kentish rag, a good effect being obtained in the interior by the way the material is worked in bands of stone and cut flints. The buttresses, which are placed at the south-west and north-west angles, are also finished off with flintwork.

I have dwelt somewhat at length on the tower, as it is the only portion of the mediæval church that has been left to us. The old tower arch could tell us much of the doings of our predecessors here. It could repeat to us the exhortation that Sir William Bulkeley, the curate, gave his flock on signing the renunciation of the Papal authority, in 1534, for the absent vicar, and the sermons of Adrian de Saravia, Abraham Colfe, Dean Stanhope and many others. It could tell us of the generations of the faithful who have gathered within the walls, in the varying costume of successive centuries, and of the old services in Latin with their elaborate ritual and costly vestments. How on Whitsun Day, 1549, Mass was said for the first time in the English tongue, and how later on, in the troublous times of Charles I, the quiet of the church was disturbed by the rough entry of the Puritan soldiers, who pulled up the newly-erected Communion-rails. These and many other episodes in the life of the people of Lewisham passed like a long panorama before the front of the old archway until, in 1774, the ancient nave gave place to the present building, and a western gallery shut off the tower from the church. Not the least of the many improvements inaugurated by Bishop Legge was the removal of this gallery and the opening to light once more of the tower archway.

VI.

Tbe Bells.

Having new-built the tower, the people of Lewisham seem to have taken the bells into consideration. And here it may not be amiss to note that the whole of the various changes, additions and the like made to the church from the earliest time of which we have record, were the work of the worshippers here. There being no resident landowner of any special importance in mediæval times, the people were thrown to a great extent on their own resources—and we have evidence that a large part of the fabric of the church itself, and the goods and ornaments thereof, were the gift of the parishioners. This applies equally to the bells. In 1517 John Francis leaves iij' vj' viij'd to buy a bell. In 1520 Stephen Levendale leaves x' for the like purpose. Other contributions occur, such as—1527, Richard Edwardes, toward a bell xl'd; 1529, Thomas Gryme, husbandman, "to the belles of Leuysham" vj' viij'd, and Denys, his widow, left iij' iiij'd "to the bell;" 1556, Cuthbert Streytt, to the reparacion of the bells vj' viij'd. Robert Batt, a member of an old Lewisham and Sydenham family, in 1535 left twelve pence to the bell frame.

When the inventory of the church goods was taken in 1552 there were in the steeple four great bells of brass. At the present time there are eight bells dating between 1766 and 1859.

No.	Inscription.	Note.	Weight.		
			cwt.	qr.	lbs.
1.	T. Mears of London, Fecit 1819	E flat.	6	1	0
2.	Lester and Pack of London, Fecit 1819 ...	D	6	2	0
3.	T. Mears of London, Fecit 1819	C	7	1	0
4.	Cast by John Warner and Sons, London, 1859. Honourable and Rev. H. Legge, D.C.L., Vicar. S. Southorn, Charles Atkins, Churchwardens. Recast 1859, by Subscriptions collected by W. S. Shove.	B flat.	8	1	8
5.	Pack and Chapman of London, Fecit 1777 ... Ye people all who hear me ring Be faithful to your God and King.	A flat.	9	1	0
6.	Cast in 1743. Jno. Baker and Geo. Thornton, Ch: Wardens. Re-cast in 1776. Paul Valentine and Jno. Evens, Ch: Wardens. Pack and Chapman of London, Fecit.	G	12	3	0
7.	Henry Corbett and Joseph Hartwell, Ch: Wardens, 1766. Lester and Pack of London, Fecit.	F	14	1	0
8. (TENOR)	This Bell was paid for by Voluntary Subscriptions, 1777. Paul Valentine and John Evens, Churchwardens. Pack and Chapman of London, Fecit.	E flat.	21	1	14

VII.

The Rebuilding in 1774.

The foregoing notes will have shown, to some extent, the condition of Lewisham Church down to the year 1773. How long before that date a feeling had spread in the place that the old church was unsuited to the requirements of a large parish and a rapidly increasing population we have no means of knowing; but at a Vestry held 16th August, 1773, it was resolved that the Right Hon. the Earl of Dartmouth, the Rev. Wm. Louth, vicar, Edward Russell, Esq., Thomas Hicks, Esq., Mr. Wm. Staples, Mr. Samuel Baughan, Mr. Paul Valentine, Mr. Henry Gresham, Mr. Charles Johnson, and the two churchwardens, Mr. John Corbett and Mr. Isaac Evans, be appointed a committee to consider the defects and want of repairs in and about the church.

The committee decided to call in professional assistance and deputed Mr. Thomas Wiggins and Mr. George Gibson, architects, to report on the building. These gentlemen, in pursuance of the order, reported that upon the most careful and mature survey they found many cracks and settlements in the Gothic piers and arches and side walls of the church; that the timber of the roof, together with the tiling, was very ruinous and in bad condition, and the pews and linings much decayed and rotted by the continual damp; that repairing it in the most substantial manner would cost the parish nine hundred pounds, and that even then they could not guarantee that the building would be free from damp. The repairs needed involved raising the floor of the church to the level of the south doors with brick arches, and paving the top of the arches to prevent the damp rising; taking down the great Gothic pier and arches on each side and carrying a truss bressemer quite across from north to south under the long bressemer, with a stone column under the same, about two feet in diameter, to support both the bressemers; taking down the gallery and re-erecting it higher on iron standards instead of wooden columns; repairing the roof where needed, making a new gutter in the middle; and altering the south doors so as to make them more convenient for the congregation to enter.

The committee not desiring to act with undue haste decided to have further advice, and Mr. John Gorham made a second survey of the interior of the church. He pronounced all the timber-work to be infected with rot, owing to the floor of the church lying considerably below the surface of the ground, and that the area which had been made on the outside, not being continued round the buttresses nor being deep enough to take the wet from the walls of the church, could have no good effect, and that the floor should be raised four feet. Mr. Gorham, being desired to take notice of the pier in the middle of the church and the arches adjoining to it, observed that they were cracked in so many places that he thought they could not con-

Lewisham Church, as rebuilt, 1774.

tinue with safety many years, and that, in order to an effectual repair of the church being made, it would be absolutely necessary that they should be taken down.

This opinion having been considered it was resolved that, inasmuch as raising the floor four feet would entail a similar elevation of the roof, it would be more advisable to build a new church.

An Act of Parliament was accordingly obtained in 1774, and the plan proposed by Mr. George Gibson for the rebuilding was approved at a Vestry held in the Vestry-room on 5th July, 1774. Tenders were invited for the rebuilding, which included the proportional raising of the tower, and that of Oliver Burton & Co. was accepted, being for the work £4,086, less £200 allowed for old material. They were, however, allowed a further sum of £110 to provide for extra security for the foundations, so that the total estimate for the work was £3,996.

A list is given in the minute-book of the trustees of all those who tendered to rebuild the church, and is as follows :—

Name.			New Church.	Old Church.		
Thos. Rawstone	...	...	£4995	£250	...	£4745
J. Piper...	...	...	4967	117	...	4850
J. Phillips	...	..	5040	200	...	4840
J. Lepard	...	...	4319	250	...	4069
J. Hall ...	...	...	4990	220	...	4770
J. Corbett *	...	...	4481	210	...	4271
J. Carpenter	...	...	4880	105	...	4775
J. Wood	...	...	5000	230	...	4770
Wm. Miller	...	...	4800	—	...	4800
R. Ruddock & Co.	...		4688	150	...	4538
J. Yallowley	...	...	4388	80	...	4308
Ben Lea	...	...	5150	... —	...	5150
J. Fox ...	...	...	4950	... —	...	4950
Fr. Carreck	...	...	4914	... 100 11s....		4813 9s.
Ol. Burton & Co.	...		4086	... 200	...	3886

The trustees were empowered under the Act to levy a rate of not more than one shilling in the pound on all land, houses, &c., in the parish—and for the more speedy accomplishing of the work to borrow a sum not exceeding £5,000 on the security of the rate. The contributors were to receive interest not exceeding 8½ per cent. The Act also authorised the letting of the vaults and of the gallery pews, the sums accruing to go towards the payment of the annuities, and, when these were paid off, towards the relief of the church rate.

The account and minute-books of the trustees for rebuilding the church escaped the fire of 1830 and are now preserved in the Vestry safe. From them we learn that the ready money to proceed with the works was obtained without much delay, and by Midsummer, 1776, had all been paid to the treasurer, Ebenezer Blackwell.

The following is a list of the contributors of the £5,000 which the Act

---

* Proposed to dig the foundation three feet below the floor of the old church.

authorised to be spent on the new church.   The entries are all in the same form, and it will suffice to give the first as a specimen:—

"Mrs. Joanna Boyle, aged 45 years, of Windmill Street, Tottenham Court "Road, in Middlesex, widow, hath paid on the 23rd day of June, 1775, unto "Ebenezer Blackwell, Esq., Treasurer to the Trustees for rebuilding the Parish "Church of Lewisham, in Kent, the sum of two hundred pounds, for which she or "her order is to be paid one annuity of fourteen pounds per annum during her natural "life by half-yearly payments, the first of which will become due on the 25th day of "December, 1775."

	Annuitant.	Age.	Residence.	Amount paid.	Annuity.
1	Mrs. Joanna Boyle ...	45...	Windmill Street, Tottenham Court Road	£200	...£14
2	Mrs. Elizabeth Biggs ...	42...	Queen Ann Street, Cavendish Square, spinster	200 ...	14
3	Mrs. Ann Jermy ...	35...	Shrewsbury, spinster ...	300 ...	21
4	Mrs. Sarah Morris ...	35...	James Street, Westminster, spinster	300 ...	19 10s.
5	Mrs. Mary Robarts ...	59...	Cirencester, Gloster, spr. ...	100 ...	8
6	Mrs. Ann Barratt ...	37...	West Ham, Essex, spr. ...	500 ...	35
7	Mr. John Bell... ...	—...	New Broad Street, London	200 ...	16
	[During the natural life of Mrs. Jane Oxnard, of Jerusalem Court, Hackney, spr., aged 56.]				
8	Mrs. Elizabeth Bull ...	59...	Hoxton, Shoreditch, wid....	200 ...	15
9	Mrs. Jane Munn ...	36..	Greenwich, spr. ...	300 ...	21
10	Mrs. Sarah Munn ...	35...	Greenwich, spr. ...	400 ...	28
11	Mrs. Martha Munn * ...	32...	Greenwich, spr. ...	300 ...	21
12	Mrs. Ann Bowyer † ...	36...	Lewisham ...	300 ...	21
13	Mrs. Ann Smith ...	36...	Camberwell ...	300 ...	21
14	Mr. John Morse ...	52...	Shipton Moyne ...	150 ...	12
15	Mrs. Mary Mewkill ...	48...	St. Aldates, Oxford, wid. ...	200 ...	16
16	Mrs. Eleonora Caroline Manger	48...	Wilhayn near Axminster, Devon	250 ...	20
17	Capt. James Miller ...	53...	St. Martin's in co. Middlesex	200 ...	16
18	Mrs. Thomasin Taylor ...	54...	St. Mary, Rotherhithe, spr.	100 ...	8
19	Mrs. Diana Hardy ...	51...	St. George, Bloomsbury, spr.	500 ...	40

£5000

The church was finished in 1777, as appears on a tablet on the south porch:

This Church was finished rebuilding
in the Year 1777
PAUL VALENTINE ⎱
and   ⎰ Churchwardens.
JOHN RUSSELL ⎰
THE REVD.
WM. LOWTH, D.D., VICAR.

* Last Annuitant. She died 10th June, 1840.
† Fourth daughter of Rev. Edward Norton, formerly of Lewisham.

Lewisham Church, c. 1876.

The first service was held on 7th September in that year. The old tower was left at the west end, but another storey was added in which the bells were hung. This was necessitated by the increased height of the church. The original nave and aisle were replaced by a building which was considered by a contemporary admirer to "do credit to the architect, Mr. Gibson, and not less to the present Earl of Dart-" mouth, whose taste dictated that elegant simplicity prevalent through the whole"— a simplicity which a later generation has failed to altogether appreciate. The new nave, which still forms the main part of the church, is a parallelogram 86 feet long by 48 feet wide (inside measurement), and had at the eastern end a small apse for the altar. On the south side a large porch with columns of the Corinthian order forms the principal entrance, and this is balanced on the north side by the parish vestry. The interior was heavily ceiled, with galleries on the north and south sides and at the west end, in which last stood the organ. The pews and fittings were all of oak, but were quite plain, except the columns on each side of the apse, which were fluted and had somewhat elaborate capitals. At the east end stood a "three decker," or clerk's box, reading pew and pulpit, with sounding board above, but on the insertion of the painted window in the apse in 1863 this was divided, the pulpit being placed on the north side, and the reading pew and clerk's seat on the south. The sounding board is now preserved in the south porch, and the panels of the pulpit form the back of the sedilia on the south side of the present chancel. Another subsequent alteration was the removal of the wooden supports to the gallery, leaving thin iron columns in their place. This was done in order to give a less heavy air to the interior, but the effect was not good, the gallery having the appearance of being supported by a row of matches.

The building even as late as 1880 was, in its general appearance and appointments, a typical "Georgian" church. The churchwardens' pew by the northern entrance, with shelves above for the weekly dole of bread for the poor—solemnly handed down after morning prayer on Sundays by the wardens and sidesmen—the high pews, and the western organ gallery with seats on either side for the school children, will be easily remembered by many parishioners.

The accompanying illustration of the interior of the eastern end of the church is from a photograph taken about 1876. Shortly afterwards the reading pew and seat for the clerk were replaced by carved oak stalls.

The old church had suffered from damp; the new very narrowly escaped destruction by fire. On the morning of 26th December, 1830, the over-heating of one of the flues set fire to the woodwork, burning some of the pews and a portion of the gallery, and damaging the ceiling. The vestry on the north side suffered most, and this is more to be deplored since it resulted in the loss of a part of the early parish registers, together with the churchwardens' account-books, &c. The injury to the church was quickly made good, but the parish records were gone beyond recall.

A further and, as it seems to me, inexcusable injury was done to the parish in the destruction of the monuments from the old church which will be found enumerated at page 6. The trustees for the rebuilding, following closely the letter of the Act, considered it to be no part of their duty to reinstate them, and after languishing for some time in the chapel of Colfe's Almshouses they were consigned to the vaults, and, with the exception of parts of those to Dr. Stanhope, Mrs. Colfe and George Hatcliff, have now disappeared.

Mr. Pery, to whose family one of the monuments was erected, applied to the trustees for leave to place a tablet in the new church, and was informed that if he elected to replace the old monument at his own cost they would charge no fees. This was the only application, so far as I can trace, from a representative of a person to whom a monument had existed. The majority of the tablets were to families doubtless long removed from the neighbourhood, and one would have thought that, even on the ground of "something to cover the bare walls," the parishioners would have gone to the trifling expense involved in their re-erection.

Of the monuments erected since the rebuilding the most noticeable is one by Flaxman to Mary, daughter of William and Paulina Lushington, who died 6th Feb., 1797, aged 26. This, originally placed on the eastern wall, is now in the north aisle below the gallery, where the churchwardens' pew formerly stood. On the left is the inscription to Dr. Stanhope. Above the north door will be found the little tablet to Mrs. Colfe, who was for "above 40 yeares a willing nurse, midwife, surgeon, "and in part physitian to all, both rich and poore."

Over the western arch is a large monument by E. H. Baily, R.A., to John Thackeray, Esq., of The Priory, a benefactor, not only to Lewisham—which is indebted to him for a row of almshouses—but also, among many other charities, to Christ's Hospital, to which he left £10,000 and his library.

The western wall above the gallery on either side is covered by large basso-relievos of white marble to the Petrie family. That on the north side is to Mrs. Ann Dick Petrie, who died 11th Feb., 1787, and is the work of Mr. Vanpook, of Brussels. It is a representation of the scene at her death, and that on the south by T. Banks, R.A., is of a similar character. They are worthy of more attention than is usually paid to them.

VIII.

The Reparations in 1881.

It now only remains to describe the alterations made in the church in 1881. In 1879 the Hon. Henry Legge, known to the villagers as "the old vicar," who had held the living for nearly half a century, resigned, and his successor, now Bishop of Lichfield, after a short interval took in hand the remodelling of the church.

The Earl of Dartmouth, the patron, defrayed the cost of building a structural chancel, in place of the apse, at the east end, the foundation stone of which was laid by the Countess of Dartmouth on 5th November, 1881. George Parker, Esq., of Lewisham House, undertook the works of the nave, which was re-opened for divine service on the 20th of the same month.

The new chancel was consecrated on Lady Day, 1882, by the Bishop of Rochester. It is 35 feet long and 22 feet 6 inches wide, and on each side is a shallow transept, that on the north containing the organ, and that on the south (which corresponds to the Chapel of the Holy Trinity in the original church) having a painted wooden screen and gallery, erected in 1888 as a memorial to the Hon. Henry Legge, with this inscription: "Henrico Legge Huius Ecclesiæ Presbytero Consanguinei Memores, MDCCCXXXI—MDCCCLXXIX." On the panels are the names of the vicars of Lewisham from the thirteenth century.

In the nave very extensive alterations were made. Wooden pillars and arches were erected, dividing the interior into a nave and aisles. The plaster ceiling was taken down, and the timber work of the roof uncovered. The western gallery was removed, thus opening to view once more the tower arch, and a flight of steps was built from the tower entrance up into the church. At the same time the high pews were replaced by open benches of oak. These alterations and the work of the chancel were carried out under the direction of Sir Arthur Blomfield, who also designed the pulpit erected by subscription in 1884 and the low screen of hammered iron placed on the top of the chancel wall in 1890.

Purists will doubtless pass a scornful verdict of "nondescript" upon the architecture of the church, yet as it stands to-day it has so much history visible in its walls that one would hesitate, and more than hesitate, before joining in a cry for a building perhaps more architecturally consistent. As we pass through the western doorway we are reminded of the patience of those "good old days" when, although within a few miles of the centre of the struggle for the Crown between the houses of York and Lancaster, our predecessors in Lewisham were content to work quietly for forty years in the new-building of the bell tower. As we ascend the western steps and enter the nave, its walls tell us of at least the outward activity of church life here in the 18th century. The new chancel and re-modelled interior of the church, with the costly mosaics and ornaments, will tell those who shall succeed us in their use that patron and parishioners at the close of the 19th century were not behind the "ages of faith" in these matters, but recognised their responsibilities and did their best to fulfil them.

IX.

The Church Windows.

As might be expected, there is no old glass in the church. The following are the subjects of such of the windows as have been filled with painted glass :—

In the Chancel.

In the eastern wall are three tall round-headed windows, and over these, in the gable, a circular window with a small round-headed light on either side. These are all filled with glass re-arranged from the windows of the old apse :—"The Magi presenting their Gifts," with an inscription, "To the blessed memory of Thomas Watson Parker, Esquire, of this Parish, and of Mary his beloved wife. Their surviving children erected this window as a token of their filial respect and love, 1863."

The south window of the sanctuary—inscribed "Born of the Virgin Mary"— represents the Babe in the Manger, with the Virgin Mother and Joseph. Inscription—"In memory of William Walter, 5th Earl of Dartmouth, who built this chancel, A.D. 1882. Born August 12th, A.D. 1826. Died August 4th, 1891." The Legge coat-of-arms is in the lower left corner.

The three windows of the gallery of the south transept represent "Faith," "Hope" and "Charity," with an inscription : "To the glory of God and in memory of Henry Legge, D.C.L., Vicar of Lewisham, 1831-1879. Died 13th Feb., 1887. This window was given by parishioners and friends."

The three windows under the said gallery represent (1) "Simeon," (2) "Christ Blessing the Children," (3) "Anna." (1) and (3) were placed by Canon Legge, to the memory of the Hon. Mrs. Henry Legge ; the centre light by General and Mrs. Lynedoch Gardiner, in memory of their three young sons, who died at Blackheath, 1854-5.

In the Nave.

On the south side of the church, under the gallery, the easternmost window represents "Christ in the midst of the Doctors," inscribed, "In memory of Robert and Mary Whomes. This window is dedicated by their son, Robert Whomes, of this Parish, 1866."

The westernmost window—"At the foot of the Cross"—inscribed, "Matri optimæ Franciscæ comitissæ de Dartmouth, Filius Henricus Legge, Ecclesiæ de Lewisham Presbyter Vicarius."

On the south side of the church, above the gallery, are four windows—the first (eastern), "St. Mary Magdalen washing the feet of Christ," inscribed, "To the glory of God. Ann Parker, died April 22nd, 1874; Thomas Parker, died Nov. 14th, 1879. This window is dedicated to the loved memory of most devoted parents by their two daughters."

The second window—"Christ feeding the Five Thousand"—inscribed, "This window is erected to the memory of George Parker, Esq., J.P., late of Lewisham House in this Parish, who died on 10th March, 1889, in his 85th year. He was a most generous benefactor to this Parish and neighbourhood and made many valuable bequests to many public Institutions. He was greatly respected and esteemed by all classes."

On the north side, under the gallery, are two windows. The easternmost represents "The Marriage in Cana," inscribed, "In remembrance of a beloved mother, by her eldest son, Benjamin Horton of this Parish, 1866."

The westernmost window contains three medallions—(1) "The Last Supper;" (2) An angel holding a scroll, "Grace and Truth came by Jesus Christ;" (3) The symbolic Bull and legend "S. Lucas."

On the north side, above the gallery, are four windows, the two eastern only containing stained glass. The first is "The Resurrection," inscribed, "To the beloved memory of Lieut.-Colonel Edward Parker, late of this Parish. This window was erected by his brother, George Parker, as a token of affection, A.D. 1867."

The next window is "The Raising of Lazarus," inscribed, "To the beloved memory of John Frederick Parker, Esquire, late of this Parish. This window was erected by his brothers, George and Edward Parker, as a token of their affection, A.D. 1866."

The west window (in the tower) is of three lights—"The Presentation in the Temple," "The Baptism of Christ," and "Christ Blessing Children"—inscribed, "This window was presented by Thomas Watson Parker, Esq., of this Parish, A.D. 1858."

When the nave was rebuilt, in 1777, a floor was inserted in the base of the tower, above the western doorway, and the space converted into a baptistry. This explains the subjects of the window. The floor was removed in 1882, and the new font, the gift of the children of the parish through the offerings at their afternoon services, placed at the top of the steps which lead up from the tower entrance.

At the west end of the nave are two windows, one under the gallery on either side :—

The northern—"The Search for the Lost Piece of Money"—(no inscription).

The southern—"The Good Samaritan." "To the glory of God and in memory of Robert Whomes of this Parish, who died July 10th, 1889, aged 74 years. This window is erected by his widow."

X.

Mosaics.

The mosaics in the chancel claim some attention. The wall spaces in the arcades above the altar and on the north side of the sanctuary were filled by Mr. John Aird in commemoration of his marriage at the parish church, whilst the remainder—intended to represent the spread of Christianity by an Empress and a Queen—was inserted in 1888, by the congregation, in memory of the Jubilee of Queen Victoria.

In the northern arcade are Rebeccah, Isaac, Sarah and Abraham. On the east wall, to the north of the altar, are Bertha, Queen of Kent, and Saint Augustine; and on the south side of the altar the Empress Helena is represented offering the Church of the Holy Sepulchre to the service of God. Over the credence is the Agnus Dei. Above the arcade on the north side is the text, "Kings shall be thy nursing fathers," and opposite to it, "Queens thy nursing mothers."

The wall space over the altar and below the eastern windows is broken by a large arched recess in the centre and two small arches on either side. The central space is filled with a cross, in brass and mosaic work, with marble bosses. The heads of the arches on the north side contain the emblems of St. Matthew and St. Mark, and on the south those of St. Luke and St. John—the spaces below the emblems being filled with a conventional design. At the back of the piscina is a small painting—"The Dead Christ"—which, a short time before the apse was taken down, had been inserted in the wall over the altar.

XI.

Chantries.

"The Chauntrye within the Parishe Churche of Lewssham was founded by one Richard Walker to the'ntent and p'pose that one preiste shulde celebrate dyvyne s'vice at an awlter within the said churche called Trynytie aulter, for the soule of the said founder and all xpen soules for ever."

So runs the heading of the certificate handed in under the Act of 1 Edward VI for the suppression of the chantries. The will of Richard Walker, founding this chantry, is of more than usual interest, on account of the detail given as to the manner in which the service was to be conducted. It is as follows:—

EXTRACT FROM THE WILL OF RICHARD WALKER.
(Prerogative Court of Canterbury, 22 Vox.)

𝔍𝔫 𝔡𝔢𝔦 𝔫𝔬𝔪𝔦𝔫𝔢, 𝔄𝔪𝔢𝔫, the xij Nov. 1494, I Richard Walker citizen and grocer of London and now parishen of the p'ishe of Levesham in Kent doo make my last wille as to my landys in London and the subberbis of the same the which were sometyme William Hobert, Bladesmyth, and the which certain persons of the Cytie of London and the p'ish of Levisham to myn use stonde enfeoffed in fee simple. The which I will yerely from hensforth shall suffre Katerin my wief and after her decesse the churchwardens of the p'ish church of Levesham, and their successours, wardeyns of the same church, to take the Rents &c. for a preste of honest and good conu'sacon dayly forto sing his masse and other Dyuyne S'uice for my soule and for the soule of my wyfe at the aultur of the trynyte chappell within the p'yshe church aforesaid. Euery Monday masse of the Angellys and eu'y Wednesday masse of the Hooly Trinite & eu'y Sat'day masse of our Lady & eu'y othur day of weke masse, and I woll he shall begynne his masse by tweine vij or viij of the clocke in the mornyng with oute a liefull cause or lettyng and also that the same preste dayly in his masse atte the first lavatarye at Sowthe ende of the aulter ther shall turne him toward the people and shall say for my sowle and the soule of my said wyf whanne she ys deceased and all cristen soulys the psalme of De profundis with the prayers and collets thervnto accustumed. And also I will the same preste twice eu'y weke that is to say upon the Wednisday & Friday shall say for my sowle and my said wyffys sowle after her decesse Placebo, Dirige and comendacion, and have yerely for his salry x^{ma} and vj' viij^d to finde him brede, wyne, and wex, to sing with as ys afore said. Also a ponne the day of the moneth that hit shall happone me to decesse to kepe within the p'ish church of Levish'm for my soule & my wyfs & for oure Frendys and all cristen soules an obite with placebo and dirige overnyght & masse of Requiem on the morow folowing by note expending yerely a boute the same obite that is to say to the prests and clerks being and helping att the same xiij' iiij^d Att which obite yerely I will that this my present wille shalbe Redde openly by fore the p'ishens there. Also I will that the vicar of the p'issh churche of Lewsham shall have yerely of the Rents ij' viij^d that is quarterly viij^d that eu'y Sonday in the pulpyte their shall haue my sowle and my wifes sowle specyally Recomended vnto the prayers of the people as the maner & custume there is vsed. The residue of profitts to be put in a chest vnder two Lokkis and two keyes to Remayne in some sure place w'in the p'ish or p'ish church aforesaid—oone kay in keping of the said p'ish church and other key of myne executors.

This will was proved 12th December, 1494. We know little of the pious founder. He tells us in another part of his will that he was born at Byngley, in Yorkshire—and he left five marcs towards the building of the steeple of Lewisham church. His arrangements, as detailed above, for the chantry were duly carried out, as appears by the certificate at its suppression. From this it would seem that the endowment consisted of

	£	s.	d.
Rent of a messuage or tenement in the Parish of Saint Martin within Ludgate London in the tenure of John Wyse of the yearly value of		liij	iiij
Rent of another tenement there in the tenure of Cristofer Harbotell	iiij	–	–
Rent of another in the tenure of John Lynne ...		lxvj	viij
In all ...	x	–	–

Whereof payments were made—	£	s.	d.
Annual tenths to the King		xiiij	–
Yearly to the Prebend of Fynsebery		xx	–
In pence at the Founder's anniversary ..		xiij	iiij
To the Vicar yearly		ij	viij
Leaving	vij	x	–

The chantry priest in 1548 was Myles North, clerk, who was 58 years of age, and it was returned that he "hath to lyve on besides the said chauntrie." The certificate further adds—

" There is not any vicar there endowed other than the vicar of the P'ishe, for that the said chauntrie is no parishe churche nor any parishe churche ther vnto appropriat and there are of houslinge people w^t in the said P'ishe——

" There hath not bene anye grammer scole kepte, preacher mayntened or pore people relevid by the said chauntrye.

"There hath not bene any sale of landes or tenements, spoyle or waste of wodes or gifte of goodes belonginge to the said chauntrye.

" Goodes there—none."

It would have been interesting to know the number of "houslinge people" in the parish at that date, an item entered in every other case, but omitted here— apparently an error on the part of the scribe.

Another chantry, that of Roger Fitz, was founded by his will dated 28th March, 1504 (P.C.C. 7 Holgrave). He was a member of an old Lewisham family whose residence, now long since disappeared, stood at Rushey Green. After desiring that he might be buried " before the middle of the Trinite awter, and that a playn stone be layd upon my body," he says :—

" Item, also I will that the lyon and the Rame beyng at the Stuys w^t in the man' of Southwarke shulde be solde and the Revenues therof comyng to purchace in London as moche londe or Rente as will fynde a p'petuall Chauntery priest syngyng for me and my frends in the forsaid churche of our Lady of Lewsham in the forme folowing, that is to say, upon Monday, Thewsday, Thursday and Satirday to syng at the awt' of the Trinite in the forsaid churche and Sonday, Wedingsday and Fryday to syng at my place in my chapell in Lewsham, at the plessur of the owners therof. Writen with myne owne hand," he adds.

This will was proved 18th April, 1504. I am not sure how far this particular bequest was acted on. The property in question—the Lyon and the Rame—was certainly not sold, as both these houses are mentioned, in the inquisition taken on the death of Sir John Fitz in 1606, as being then part of the family property. No mention is made in the Chantry Certificates of this chantry, and it would consequently seem as though, either it was not proceeded with, or that some other arrangement was made.

These chantries—in common with others of a similar nature—were suppressed by the Act of 1 Edward VI, and the lands and endowments seized into the king's hands.

XII.

Gilds.

Among the many interesting features of the parochial life of the middle ages are the gilds or brotherhoods which existed not only in the large towns but also in country districts. They consisted of both men and women, who bound themselves to observe certain rules. These were, usually, to attend the meetings of the fraternity and the funerals of its members, and to pay a small subscription, the fund so raised going to the relief of members who were out of work through no misbehaviour on their part, or who were incapacitated by age or illness from earning their own living. The gild would also look to the light of its patron saint in the church.

There were two such fraternities in connection with Lewisham Church—one called the Brotherhood of Our Lady and Saint George, and the other the Brotherhood of the Holy Trinity.

The Brotherhood of the Holy Trinity was the older and more important gild, and I find the following bequests to it, with others of a like nature :—

1471. By William Sprigg, a cow.

1473 „ William Scott vj^d.

1476. „ John Gwyn vi^s viij^d for making his grave in the Trinity chapel.

1476. „ Christian Sprigg, widow, iij^s iiij^d to the sustentation of the fraternity.

1509. By John Smyth, a bullock price iiij^s to the fraternity, "and I will the same be paid to the wardens of the same 'ad incremento.'"

1511. „ Richard Chybnall—To the Bretherhod of the Trinite xij^d.

1511. „ John A Wynne—To the Fraternity of the Holy Trinity iij^s iiij^d.

1514. „ Thomas Rede, "I will the Trenyte gilde in Leuysham have a stere of on yere age."

The other gild was not founded until well on in the sixteenth century—at least the first notice I have found of it is in 1527, when Richard Edwardes left xl^d "to the brotherhed of Our Lady and Saynt George," and in 1528 John Berepikyll, husbandman, left xij^d "to the brotherhod of ou^r lady and Saynt George in the saide my p'issh church."

The name of this gild may possibly survive in the George Inn—though not in its present position. In days gone by (as far back as Elizabeth's reign) what is now called Zion House was known as The George, and from its proximity to the church it is not unlikely that it may have been the meeting hall of this brotherhood.

Both of these fraternities were—we may assume—suppressed by the Act of 1 Edward VI, if they had not been dissolved previously. No later notice of either of them occurs. They were not endowed with any lands.

XIII.

Images and Lights in the Church before the Reformation.

No account of the mediæval church would be complete without some reference to the images and lights which existed prior to the Reformation. The never-failing sources of information on these subjects are the wills of the faithful departed, and this section is entirely compiled from those to be found either in the Prerogative Court of Canterbury or the Consistory Court of Rochester.

There were at least two images of the Blessed Virgin in the church, one in the high chancel, the other in the body of the church, and before these were the usual lights kept burning. These were contributed to by the devoutly disposed from time to time. Thus, in 1459, William Batt left a small sum to the light of the blessed Mary. In 1473 Cecily, wife of John Lamkyn of Perrystrete, left viij^d towards painting the image of the Virgin, and in 1476 John Gwyn left xij^d towards painting the image of the blessed Mary next the high altar. In 1513 Sir John Aschley, curate, left a taper to burn before Our Lady in the chancel; and there are many similar bequests. The image of the Virgin in the body of the church stood on one of the pillars on the south side of the nave. Thomas

Hawkyns in 1501 left a taper of the value of ij^d "to o' lady in the wall at Lewsam." In 1512 Richard Batt of Sippenham left a taper of wax of half a pound weight to the light of our Lady standing on the south side of the body of the church, perpetually to be founden by his heirs "to bren on the Sondaies and festival daies." In 1524 Thomas Johnson, yoman, left iiij^d to our Lady's light before his pew in the church. Another seat-holder hard by was one John Kichell, who in 1514 left xij^d "to our Lady light on the pilour at my sete end."[*] Canterbury pilgrims will doubtless remember a similar pillar with a canopied niche in the church of Saint Alphege in that city. In the body of the church was an altar of our Lady, at which Stephen Levendale, who died in 1520, and who desired to be buried before the Rood, wished mass to be sung, and left five marks therefor.

Another light was an oil lamp, generally alluded to by the people as "the light called the Basin light," to the sustentation of which most persons left a donation. Its position is nowhere mentioned. It may have hung before the high altar, or, perhaps more probably, before the great crucifix over the beam.

In 1471 Peter Toller left iiij^d "to the common light for the dead in the body of the church." Although a very usual light in some parts of the country under various names, this is the only mention I have found in connection with Lewisham, unless the "Basin" light referred to above was its ordinary name here. In West Kent generally it was called the "herse" light, and from expressions used in some of the Rochester Consistory wills I gather that it was the light or lights placed about the hearse during the burial or commemoration service.

There was also the usual light burning before the rood which stood over the entrance of the chancel. This is called the "light of the Holy Cross" by John Shott in 1484, "the light before the image of the crucified" in John Gwyn's will in 1476, "the beem light" by Richard Howchenson in his will dated 1500, and "the Rood Light" by Robert Cheseman in 1498, who left iij^s iiij^d thereto.

In the Trinity Chapel was the light of the Holy Trinity, and there was also an image of Saint John Baptist, before which John Gwyn in 1476 desired to be buried. Robert Cheseman in 1498, besides wishing to be interred before the same, further charged his executors "to fynde two Tapers of wax to bren before the image of Saynt Baptiste." To the lights of the Trinity and Saint John in 1533 John Stake left a bequest.

For a short time there was another light in the church in memory of King Henry VI. It is mentioned but once here, in the will of Thomas Johnson, who died in 1524 and left iiij^d to the same; but the people regarded their unfortunate sovereign as a saint, and mention of images of him is not uncommon.

---

[*] In 1594 John Soane, tanner, left instructions that he was to be buried in the parish church of "Lewsham, as near the accustomed place where I sate in the same church."

All the lights before images were taken away in the reign of Edward VI, under whose injunctions only two were to remain, viz., on the high altar before the Sacrament; and even these went after a time, and were only replaced here in 1882.

XIV.

The Ornaments of the Church and of the Ministers thereof.

Besides keeping the lights before the Saints and assisting in the fabric of the church, the parishioners were ever ready to provide those things necessary for the due performance of divine service.   In 1521 Stephen Colman left the residue of his goods towards the purchase of a "payre of organys," unless the churchwardens thought something else would be more desirable.   His suggestion seems, however, to have been followed, as in 1552 we find a "payre of organs " in the inventory of the church goods.*

Bequests of books for the various offices were by no means uncommon.   In 1471 William Sprigg, the munificent founder of the tower works, further charged his executors to purchase a portifor of the value of twelve marcs, which should remain in the choir before the vicar for ever.   Thomas Baker in 1521 left money for the purchase of a grayll.

Other ornaments left to the church were a banner valued at xiij^s iiij^d left by John Francis in 1517, cloth for a canopy with four staves left by Richard Skipwith in 1522, etc., etc.

In 1527 William Berepikle, who desired five masses of the Five Wounds of Our Lord to be sung for him, left iij^s iiij^d to the reparation of the best cross, or else a herse cloth to be bought.

With regard to vestments, in 1506 Thomas Batt in his will says "yf the churchwardens or any other well disposed persones wilbey a nue cope or vestyment to honor God w^t in the said church thereto I geve xx^d." John Robyns, who died in 1511, left to the church a vestment of white damask, with all necessaries thereto belonging, " to thon^r of the holy Trinity and o^r Lady."

Some interesting bequests were made of stuff for altar cloths.   In 1512 William Batt left cloth of the value of xiij^s iiij^d to hang before the altar.   In 1544 Isabella Fleming, widow of Roger Fitz, who founded one of the chantries in the

---

* When the church was taken down in 1774, arrangements were made for the safe custody of the then existing organ with a view to its re-erection in the new building.   Samuel Spencer, Esq., J.P., about 1790, presented the church with a larger instrument which had the donor's arms thereon—Quarterly argent and gules, in 2nd and 3rd quarters a fret of the first; over all a bend sable charged with 9 plates—but it was in its turn replaced by another, erected by public subscription.   This last, which stood like its two predecessors in the western gallery, was removed with the gallery in 1881, and the present organ, built by Messrs. Brindley & Foster of Sheffield, placed in the northern transept of the new chancel.

church and whose house stood at Rushy Green, left her kirtle of crimson satin to the church to be made into a vestment. She also willed that an altar cloth should be made of her damask jacket of white and green for the high altar. Bequests of this nature are of value as giving a probable clue to the presence in the church inventories of cloths and vestments of colours scarcely authorized by the rubrics.

Sir John Aschley, curate of Lewisham, who died in 1513, left a gold ring towards making a pix, and also a surplice to the church, with a satchel in which to keep it.

When a full inventory of the ornaments of the church was made in the sixth year of Edward VI (1552), Lewisham Church was very rich in both plate and vestments which had gradually accumulated by purchase and gifts such as those stated above.

Inventory of Church Goods.
The Hundred of Blackheath.
LEWYSHAM xvi Nov. vi Ed. vi (1552).
RICHARD DYNGLY and RICHARD HOWLETT gent, churchwardens.

This Inventorie indented (? made) the vi daye of Novembre in the sixte year of the raigne of our soveraigne lord Edwarde the Sixteth, by the grace of God &c. Between Sir Percyvall Harte and Sir Marten Bowes Kts John Browne and Thos Lovelace Esquires, comyssioners amongst others authorised by virtue of his Graces comyssion—bering teste at West^m xvi daye of Maie in the sixt yeare of his most gracious reigne, for the viewe, presentment, and certificate of all the goodes, plate, juells, bells, and ornaments in every churche or within the said countie of Kent belonging or in anywise apperteyning to them and others directed and allotted to the hundreds of Blackheath, Bromley, Beckenham, &c. &c. within the said countie of Kent of the one part, and Richard Dingley and Richard Howlett gent churchwardens of the p'rishe Church of Lewisham aforesaide of the other p^{te}, witnesseth that the said Comyssioners have delivered by these p'ntes to the said churchwardens all the p'celle herein particularly wrytten.

First ij chalics with their patents of silver wherof the best with the patent double gilte weying xxiij oz thother with the patent weying xiiij ounces di.

Item one pix of silver waying xiiij ounces.

Item one clothe of silke to hang over the pix.

Item one hanginge for thalter of damaske yelowe & blewe.

Item one pair of curteynes of yelowe and blew taffitay.

Item one payr of curteyns of the same to the highe alter.

Item iiij alter clothes of lynnen.

Item one cope of blewe velvett, one vestment of blewe silke with all other things thereto belonging of the same.

Item ij coopes of blewe silke imbrodred with golde, with a vestment and thapparell thereto belonging with deacon and subdeacon of the same.

Item one old grene cope of silke.

Item one vestment of whit saten with all that belongith therto.

Item one vestment of white chamlett with all that belongith thereto.

Item one vestment of red velvett for the Lente.

Item one vestment of blewe silke imbrothered with gold with all thinges thereto belonging.

Item one other of red silke with all things thereto belonging.

Item one blake vestment with a red bake with all things thereto belonging.

Item ij old silke vestments.

Item ij clothes of silke thon called the Canapie thother the Care clothe.

Item the herse clothe of blake damaske.

Item iij payre of censers of latten.

Item iij payre of latten candlesticks and ij basons and on ewer of latten.

Item ij holy water stoppes of latten, one chrysmatory of latten.

Item one shippe of latten to putt in frankyncense.

Item ij silke pillowes one without a covering.

Item one crosse of latten with ij clothes of grene silke.

Item ij surplesses and ij rochetts and one diaper towell of lynnen.

Item ix houselyng towels of lynnen and v amyces.

Item xii corporax cases, and vi clothes to the same ij whereof embrothered with golde, thother of silke.

Item one paire of white curtens and ij Tables of Alblaster pictured with images.

Item ij bibles and one paraphrasis of Erasmus.

Item iij sepulcre clothes of lynnen.

Item one clothe for the same of sylke.

Item vj chists.

Item ij banner clothes of lynnen paynted.

Item one sute of Lenten clothes of white spotted with red.

Item on vale clothe, pictured with the Passion, of lynnen with redd spots.

Item one funt cloth of lynnen.

Item iij clothes to hang over Santes of lynnen cloth.

Item ij payre of curteyns for the same of lynnen.

Item iij basens for lyghts to be sett upon in the churche.

Item xix candlesticks of pewder.

Item ij cruetts of pewder, one paire of organes.

Item iiij greate bells of brass sutyed in the steple.

Item one sants bell of brasse called the morowmas bell.

Item on hand bell and ij sacrying bells of brass.

To be safely kept and preserved by the saide churchwardens and the same and every p'celle thereof to be forth comying at all times hereafter when it shall be of them required, in witness wereof as well the said commissioners as the said churchwardens have subscribed their names on the daye and yeare above written.

PERCYVALL HARTT   MARTYN BOWES

JNO BROWNE   THOMAS LOVELACE

RICHARD DYNGLEY   RICHARD HOWLETT

Mem: Endorsed at Estgrenwich same date. All goodes in the inv^{try} of iii Ed. vi are in this and are now to be delivered to the churchwardens excepte ij corporax cases one Rochett ij pair of old . . . . of Redd & green saye presented to be stolen.

From the above it will be seen that in 1552 the church plate consisted of :—

A chalice with the paten, of silver double gilt, 23 oz.

A chalice with paten 14½ oz.

A pix of silver weighing 14 oz.

These were probably sold early in Elizabeth's reign to buy larger communion cups.

Henry Brooke of London, mercer, who was buried at Lewisham, in his will dated 1586 desired " that a Communion cup of silver and parcel guilte, and a plate trencher of silver shalbe gieuen unto the parrishe of Lewsham to continue for ever." If this bequest was carried out, the cup has certainly not " continued for ever," none of the present plate being so old.

Canon Scott Robertson, in his " History of the Church Plate of Kent," tabulates the result of the inquiry in 1735 by the Archdeacon of Rochester (Arch. Cant. vol. xvi), and it appears that at that date Lewisham returned as follows :—

			ozs.	dwts.
Cup, one silver	...	...	17	19
Flagon, one silver	...	...	59	4
" "	...	...	57	2
Paten, one silver	...	...	20	2
Almsdish "	...	...	15	10
A silver spoon	...	...	1	10

These are all still in the possession of the church, as shown in the following inventory of church goods, 1892.

LEWISHAM, 1st of JULY, 1892.

THOMAS ALFRED WARRINGTON and ROBERT HARDY SMITH, churchwardens.

An Inventory of the goods, plate and ornaments in the Parish Church of Lewisham, made the day and year above written.

First. A silver-gilt chalice, weighing 17 ozs. 19 dwts., inscribed " Given to the Parish Church of Lewisham at Easter, A.D. 1686." Hall-mark 1684.

A silver-gilt chalice, weighing 20 ozs., inscribed "Lewisham Church, A.D. 1806." Hall-mark 1806.

A silver-gilt paten on a raised base, weighing 20 ozs. 2 dwts., inscribed "This belongs to the Parish of Lucham." Hall-mark of 1718.

A silver-gilt paten, originally an alms-plate, weighing 15 ozs. 10 dwts., inscribed "This belongs to the Parish of Lucham." Hall-mark 1685. It was given to the church in 1686.

A silver-gilt flagon, weighing 59 ozs. 2 dwts., inscribed "Given to y᷎ Parish Church of Lewisham at Easter, A.D. 1686." Hall-mark 1640.

A silver-gilt flagon, weighing 57 ozs. 4 dwts., inscribed "Given to the Parish Church of Lewisham at Easter, A.D. 1686." Hall-mark 1640.

A silver-gilt perforated spoon, 1 oz. 10 dwts. It is marked R⸳O, and on the top $\frac{R}{1716}$.

> The gift of the Rev. Hon. Henry Legge, vicar.

A bread-knife with a handle of Chinese work. The blade is English, hall-marked—S—and the makers' names, J.A., I.A.

> The gift of the Rev. Hon. Henry Legge, vicar.

A silver bowl, weighing 36 ozs. 10 dwts., inscribed "The gift of Thomas Hawtree of Deptford to the Parish Church of Lewisham in Kent 1735." Hall-mark 1735, and the makers' initials, R.G., T.C.

A paten, silver and gilt, weighing 7 ozs. 10 dwts., from a Russian church. Inscription in Slavonian, "Behold the Lamb of God," &c. It is engraved with the picture of a chalice with Child lying therein and two attendant angels holding staves; above is a Glory from which proceeds the Dove. Inscribed "Lewisham Parish Church, Easter 1887."

> The gift of the Rev. Hon. Augustus Legge, vicar.

A silver-gilt almsdish, weighing 14 ozs. 5 dwts. Inscribed "Lewisham Parish Church Easter 1885." It is ornamented in repoussé work, and in the centre is a shield with the arms of the See of Rochester. Above the helmet and mantling is a crest—a peacock.

> The gift of the Rev. Hon. Augustus Legge, vicar.

A further set of communion vessels, for use at week-day celebrations, consisting of (1) a small silver paten on a raised base, inscribed "Lewisham Parish Church 1891," (2) a small silver chalice, plain, with the same inscription, weighing 12 ozs. 11 dwts., (3) a glass flagon with electro-plated mountings.

> The gift of the Rev. Hon. Augustus Legge, vicar.

Two silver staves, for use by the churchwardens on festival days, each surmounted by a mitre charged with the arms of the See of

Rochester and the Virgin and Child on one side, and the Virgin and Child and crossed swords on the other. The inscription on each is "Presented by Robert Whomes 1868. Charles Atkins and Thos. H. Furze, churchwardens, 1868." Each is fitted with a silver handle and with an ebony staff. Hall-mark 1843 and 1848 respectively.

Two oak staves surmounted by a ball and cross, which stand by the churchwardens' seats at other times.

A pair of large candlesticks of brass, which stand upon the altar.

Five pairs of flower vases of brass of various sizes, which stand upon the ledge above the altar.

> The gift of Mr. and Mrs. Kenward.

One super-frontal of black velvet embroidered ; in continual use.

One frontal to the altar of white silk embroidered ; for use on festival days.

Another frontal of dark red silk powdered with passion flowers; for use in Advent and Lent.

Another frontal of red silk with panels on either side of blue, embroidered ; for use at other times than the above.

A book-desk of brass on a raised stand ; for use upon the altar.

> The gift of Mr. W. Dunston.

Two surplices for the clergy, 69 for men and boys in the choir, and 49 cassocks.

Three stoles of white silk embroidered for use on Festival days and three of red silk for use at other times.

Six sets of book markers of white silk and red silk for use at the seasons above-named.

Two linen clothes to cover the table of the altar at Communion time.

Three sets of altar linen each consisting of

| 1 Burse | 1 Corporal | 1 Fair linen cloth |
| 1 Linen Chalice veil embroidered, | | 1 Linen Veil & 2 Purificators |

A large brass eagle lectern—inscribed "St. Mary's Lewisham 1877. Dono dedit Henricus Legge, Presbyter."

A brass ewer to the font.

> The gift of the Hon. Mrs. Henry Legge.

A desk of wood from which the Litany is sung, and which stands at the foot of the chancel steps, with cloths for the same, one of white silk, one of red silk, and another of dark red silk embroidered with passion flowers for use as stated above.

> The gift of the Rev. C. J. Palmer, curate.

Another desk of wood, which stands before the sedilia on the south side of the sanctuary.

The gift of the Rev. Hon. Augustus Legge, vicar.

A desk of brass upon the pulpit.

The gift of Thomas Alfred Warrington and Thomas Howard Lavers, churchwardens.

An old chair of oak, carved, standing on the north side of the sanctuary, for use by the Bishop when he visits the church, with a desk before the same.

Two other chairs like the foregoing, one standing in the south transept —or vicar's pew—and the other in the churchwardens' vestry.

There are also belonging to the church the usual office books, a great Bible on the lectern, music books for the choir, &c.

XV.

The Parish Registers.

The fire in the vestry in 1830 has already been referred to. The registers and other documents were kept in an iron chest, but this was doubtless soon over-heated and all the parochial papers and a large portion of the registers perished. Unfortunately scarcely any transcripts are available at Rochester, but copies kept by the parish clerk from 1700, and other notes, make the register from that date fairly perfect.

Such portions as now exist from 1558 to 1750 were printed in 1891, and as a complete account of the books is given in the preface to that work, it will be unnecessary to deal any further with the matter here, except to quote one entry in the burial register for 1560 (preserved for us by Mr. Lysons).

On the 12 day May was buried, marke that well,
a man from Pigeons of the south end
They did not him know nor where he did dwell
Charity to lodg him did me compell.

XVI.

The Churchyard.

The churchyard, which contains 1a. 2r. 27p., has been enlarged on two separate occasions—firstly, in 1791, when a piece of land containing 1r. 33p. was, with the consent of the Patron and Vicar, taken from the Church Meadow on the north-western side ; and secondly, in 1817, when a piece containing 1r. 16p., on the north-eastern side next Lewisham House, was added.

Until the cemetery at Brockley was formed the Parish Churchyard was, of course, the only burial ground, and the number of interments there must be very large.*

The burials in Elizabethan times averaged 30 to 40 yearly, rising to 100 in plague years, and in the eighteenth century alone about seven thousand are recorded in the registers.

The oldest existing stone is a flat slab near the wall of the south chancel with this inscription—

> Here lyeth the body of
> Abraham Clowder, who
> departed this life the
> 2 day of November, 1686.

The tomb—in the western portion of the yard—of Thomas Dermody, who died in 1802 at the early age of 28, should be visited by those of a poetical turn of mind; a verse from one of his own poems is inscribed thereon. The obelisk on the northern side is to the Blackwell family, of "The Limes"—the friends of the Wesleys—and hard by are the tombs of Mr. Inglis and Mr. Lowth, former vicars. Another interesting monument is that to the How family, who owned the mill at Southend where, so we are informed, "the art of cutlery was improv'd, and carry'd on to the greatest perfection." This tomb is by the north side of the tower, and has the How coat-of-arms—a fess between three wolves' heads, impaling three fleurs-de-leuses—well cut on the top.

The wills of parishioners yield a little information as to the churchyard. We learn, for instance, that the burial place of the Batt family, once very numerous in Lewisham and Sydenham, was by the chancel head. In 1527 Richard Edwardes desired to be buried "betuene the belfree and the u (*i.e.*, yew) tree there," and in 1542 John Stake expressed his wish to be buried "under the ewe tree." The practice of planting yews in churchyards has been so frequently written upon that I need do no more than allude to it here. In one of the parish books appear the following notes regarding those in this yard :—

"In memmorandum—in the year 17¹¹ in February was The Yew tree planted at the west end of the curch Giuen by Mrs. Soulsby then Liueing at The Lyon and Lamb at the lower end of the town in Remembrance of Her husband Thomas Holmbes—planted by Mr. John Spencer then clerk, and John Phillips, Sʳ John Lethieulliers Gardenner."

"The other yew tree in March the year following 17¹⁴/₁₅—In Remembrance of John Phillips the aforesaid Gardenner, Raised by him and planted by the sucseding gardennar—according to his own will and apointment."

---

* The churchyard was closed from 1st June, 1855, by an Order in Council dated 13th Sept., 1854; but the new cemetery not being ready, the time was extended to 1st March, 1856, by an Order in Council dated 7th Dec., 1855.

Both these trees are now gone—the latter was cut down in 1881, when the new chancel was built.

In the churchyard formerly stood two parochial institutions, the cross and the stocks. In 1523 the cross had fallen into disrepair, and Adam Momforth in his will left xx⁴ towards the erection of a new one. The burial register 173⁰ contains the following: "Feb 23 Sarah Saunders Mr. Barnes' servant, in yᵉ middle of yᵉ Plat next "yᵉ Stocks." Village cross and stocks have alike disappeared, and for many years the yard had a deserted appearance; but now gravelled walks and flower beds give a cared-for aspect to the ground, and there are seats for those disposed to linger. Surely if there is any spot in this rapidly changing parish which will help us in recalling the past, it is the old churchyard—the long home of many a sturdy Kentish yeoman and peasant, so many of whom helped, as best they might, to add somewhat to the fabric and ornament of their parish church, and (unconsciously) made that history which it is now our delight to study and unfold—

Requiem æternam dona eis, Domine,
Et lux perpetua luceat eis.

XVII.

The Vicarage House.

In the volume for 1842 of the "Messager des Sciences Historiques de Belgique" will be found a very interesting précis of documents in the archives of East Flanders which touch upon English matters. Many of them relate to Lewisham, and bear witness to the trouble the Abbot of St. Peter's at Ghent had to retain his property. No. 18 of the series is an agreement, made in 1218, between the Bishop of Rochester and the Abbot, regarding the churches of Greenwich and Lewisham, their tithes, &c., and in this it was laid down that "the vicar of Lewisham ought to be properly housed." A perpetual vicar had only just begun to be appointed to the place, and the "chaplains" who had hitherto served the church doubtless lodged at the Priory.

The vicarage is mentioned in documents from time to time, but there is nothing to show whether it occupied its present position. Abraham Colfe was too busy with his schemes for the Grammar School to tell us about his own dwelling, and the destruction of the parish papers in 1830 leaves us in considerable doubt on this as on many other points.

Of one fact, however, we are certain, and that is that we owe the present vicarage-house to Dr. Stanhope, who was appointed to the living in 1689. In 1692

The Vicarage=house, Lewisham.

he pulled down the old house, and clearing away the rubbish, proceeded to rebuild. He has, in his diary, left a complete account of the cost, which he apparently defrayed himself, and which is as follows:—

		£	s.	d.
1692.	Pd for Serving and Return of the Comn of View	00	15	0
1693.	For faculty to build, Entry &c.	02	17	10
	& Comn under Seal & For pulling down the old House & making good fences	07	4	0
	For clearing Rubbish and digging the Foundations	03	10	0
	To Mr. Moore for Timber	56	10	0
	Pd for 70000 Place Bricks ... ... ⎫ 10000 Stock Bricks ... ... ⎬ and 2000 Rubbing Bricks ... ... ⎭ to Mr. Nich. Goodwin of Hamersmith	54	06	0
	To Bricklayers in part	61	16	6
	More to Bricklayers	18	10	0
	More for Bricks	23	0	0
	More for Timber	27	0	0
	To Carpenters for work on my House ...	82	16	6
	To Sawyers	11	02	0
	To Plaisterers	40	10	0
	To Stonecutter	27	05	0
	To the Lime Man	30	00	0
	For Sand & Carriage	03	09	0
	For Laths Nails & Tilepins	06	05	0
	For 2700 & half of Tiles	02	15	0
	To the Joyner	48	16	0
	To the Blacksmith	22	10	0
	To the Locksmith	03	19	0
	To the Glasier	15	10	0
	To the Plumber	26	12	8
	To the Painter	25	05	0

Besides many other Bills mislaid or lost. The totall which I find summd up from Particulars not to be found amounts to £739 13 0.

	£	s.	d.
Repairs of Vicaridge Barn to Carpenter	18	10	0
Paleing to my Garden and yard	47	10	0
For making my garden— For workmanship	10	12	0
For Turf, Gravel Sand, Seeds, Trees & Setting & laying ...	42	06	6

In 1692 the making of my garden and the fence of that and the yard stood me in £114 9 0½.

In this year the building the base of my house and the Brick wall to the Street stood me in £653 0 0.

1693. In this year the finishing of my house stood me in £315 0 0. The repairs of my Barn and Stables in £28.

1700. May. Altering the chimney in the little Parlour £00 07 4.

1718. Nov. 12. Pᵈ to John Finch of Deptford for clay for raising my Kitchin
    pavemt £01 05 0.
1719. Sept. To Mr. Gilham for wainscotting my study below stairs £04 06 0
    For other repairs and improvements of my house ... 06 03 0
1723. Memorand : That my wife did out of her allowance for the year 1723 pay
    to the Bills of Bricklayers, Carpenters, &c., for the Repairs and
    Improvements of my Vicarage house at Lewisham more than £70 0 0.

The house thus erected has been the home of the vicars of Lewisham since
Dean Stanhope's time, except during the vicariate of the Hon. Henry Legge, who
lived at Holly Hedge House, on Blackheath, when the vicarage was occupied at
first by one of the curates (Mr. Morgan), and afterwards was let. On the appointment of the Hon. A. Legge in 1879, the house was renovated and enlarged by the
addition of a drawing-room and other apartments on the garden side ; but the front
to the High Street presents practically the same appearance as when first built.
The accompanying illustration is from a photograph taken in 1880.

XVIII.

Glebe Land, &c.

In 1650 the Vicarage of Lewisham was returned as worth £120 per annum,
and the house and 54 acres of glebe land were worth besides £50 per annum.

At the end of Dr. Stanhope's diary of accounts is the following terrier of the
glebe :—

"A survey of the Glebe Land belonging to the Vicaridge of Lewisham in the
County of Kent carefully taken by admeasurem¹ in the year 1714.

	ACR.	KD.	P.
"The meadow next the churchyard	2	3	9
The meadow next beyond on the other side the River ...	3	3	27
The alder next beyond that	3	1	21
A small Inclosure under Vicars-hill	0	3	0
The West side of Vicars hill next to the Wood	10	0	0
The North side of Vicars Hill (the Shaw new grubbᵈ up being included)	2	2	24
The further Field under the Hill, N-East	8	3	25
The nearer Field under the Hill, S-E.	7	2	2
The little Meadow next Brockley High-way	2	0	27
The Middle Meadow	6	1	8
The farthest Meadow North	3	3	27
A little Island by the Mill	1	1	0
In all	63	2	10

"Extract from the Registry of Rochester.

"A copy of part of the Terrar for Lewisham Vicarige given in by Mr. Abraham Colf at Arch-Bishop Laud's primary Visitation which is as follows :—

"'Also the Vicar hath no Tithe Corn, but he hath all the Tithe of Wood, Hay, Lamb and Wool and all other smaller Tithes, except Hay of the Lords-p. Only the owners of Colaton's Copice have the Two last Falls kept back the Tithe.'"

At the apportionment of rent charge in lieu of tithes in 1845, the Glebe was made up as follows :—

Occupier.	No. on Plan.	Name of Land, &c.	Nature.	A.	R.	P.
Morgan, Evan	... 1350 ...	Vicarage House ...	—— ...	0	3	38
Penn, John	... 1297a ...	Glebe	Garden ...	0	1	0
	1840 ...	——	Pasture ...	1	2	33
Owen, Abraham	... 1370 ...	Church Meadow ...	Pasture ...	2	0	17
	1834 ...	Further Field ...	,, ...	3	3	16
	1835 ...	Middle Field ...	,, ...	3	1	15
Russell, Joseph	... 1838 ...	——	Pasture ...	2	0	37
Willmott & Co.	... 1839 ...	——	,, ...	4	1	24
Selby, Wm.	... 1841 ...	——	,, ...	6	0	21
	1844 ...	——	,, ...	10	1	36
	1845 ...	Vicars Hill ...	,, ...	14	2	36
	1846 ...	——	,, ...	8	2	7
	1848 ...	——	,, ...	3	3	25
Grubb, Henry	... 1847 ...	——	Pasture ...	2	2	24
Several Parties	... 2646 ...	——	,, ...	6	3	38
			Total ...	72	1	7

It was also declared that the Right Hon. the Earl of Dartmouth, the improprietor, hath the tithe of Corn and Grain and the Vicar all other tithe.

The apportionment was declared to be :—

	£	s.	d.
Tithe rent charge payable to the Vicar	1006	19	6
,, ,, ,, to the Improprietor ...	420	3	9
	1427	3	3

Since the above date some portions of the glebe have been sold for the Recreation Ground, Railways, etc. (Nos. 1834, 1835, etc.) The greater part of the remainder is now being built over.

The Parliamentary Return of Glebe Lands made in 1886 gave that belonging to St. Mary's, Lewisham, as 60a. 2r. 28p., and the gross estimated rental at that date to be £227 10s.

The estimated gross income of the benefice for the year 1891, as given in Crockford's Clerical Directory, was £1261, and is thus made up :—

	£
Tithe Rent Charge, £636, average	515
60 Acres of Glebe, rental of	416
Court of Chancery	72

(Derived from the sale of portions of the Glebe lands to the South Eastern Railway for their Main and Mid Kent Lines).

		£
Queen Anne's Bounty		148
(From certain redemptions of tithe).		
Ecclesiastical Commissioners		50
(From sums received from the sale of portions of the Glebe lands under the Act of 1886).		
Fees		60
	Gross Income ...	...£1261

From this must be deducted the various charges, taxes, etc., estimated to leave a net income of £753.

The Vicars of Lewisham
and their Curates.

The Vicars of Lewisham.

The dates of institution and other notes regarding the vicars have been obtained from Brit. Mus. Add. MSS. 11819, 11820, and 31979 folios 283-5 (being extracts from the Rochester Episcopal Registers, by Archdeacon Denne). These are supplemented by Newcourt's "Repertorium," Foster's "Alumni Oxonienses" (to which I am much indebted), &c.

GEFFREY,

 Chaplain of Lievesham, appears as one of the witnesses to an arrangement, made about 1200, regarding the appointment of a priest to the Church of St. Alphege, Greenwich. (Messager des Sciences Historiques de Belgique, 1842, p. 238, &c.)

ROBERT,

 Vicar of the Church of Lievesham, is witness to an instrument appointing one Nicholas to the Church of Greenwich, dated at Bromley, February, 1239. (Messager des Sciences Historiques de Belgique, 1842, p. 238, &c.)

RICHARD,

 Vicar on the Feast of St. Michael the Archangel, 1267. (Reg. Temp. Roffen, fo. 24a).

WILLIAM AYNO.

 The date of his institution is not known. He resigned in 1321 and is stated to have gone to Hornsey; but there is no record of his having been inducted to that living. In 1327 he resigned Horndon-on-the-hill, Essex (Lond. Reg. 64 Baudake). He was also vicar of High Roding, but in 1325 exchanged to Farnham, Essex, to which he was instituted 5th Non. March, 1325 (ibid fo. 61). In 1328, however, he again exchanged back to High Roding, being re-instituted 2nd Non. Dec., 1328 (ibid fo. 66).

RALPH DE OLNEYE.

He was vicar of Haringeye (Hornsey), which he resigned in 1321 and was presented to Lewisham by James de Doura, Prior of Lewisham and Procurator of the Abbot and Convent of St. Peter of Ghent, being instituted 18th Dec., 1321. (Register of Hamo de Hethe, fo. 52a and 65b). He was vicar here on 19th Oct., 1324 (ibid fo. 90a).

JOHN DE LEE.

Instituted 10th Jan., 1327 (Reg. Hamo de Hethe, fo. 75b), by the patron, James de Doura, Prior of Lewisham, as before. He was vicar of Lewisham until 1345, when he exchanged to Stepney. In 1352 he, with others at Stepney, had the King's licence to give a messuage, &c., to the Master and Brethren of St. Thomas, Southwark (Pat. 26 E. iii, p. 3).

JAMES PUNDRICK

Was vicar of Stebbunhith, or Stepney, but exchanged with John de Lee, and was admitted to the vicarage of Lewisham 9th March, 1345 ; patron, James de Doura, Prior of Lewisham, as before. (Reg. Hamo de Hethe, fo. 222a). He was vicar here 7th Jan., 1347 (ibid 272a).

THOMAS TWENGHE.

Presented by King Edward III, the vicarage being in the hands of the Crown owing to the war with France. He was admitted 4th Dec., 1353. (Reg. John de Scapeia, fo. 260a). He was vicar of Lewisham for only a few months, and in the spring of 1354 exchanged to Wodeberghe, in the diocese of Sarum.

JOHN DE KENDALE.

He was rector of Wodeberghe, in the diocese of Sarum, but exchanged with Thomas Twenghe and was admitted vicar of Lewisham 24th May, 1354. (Reg. John de Scapeia, fo. 261b).

[A priest of this name was admitted to the rectory of Alhallows, Lombard-street, London, 6th Id. Nov., 1351 (London Register, 259 Islip), and resigned in 1353 (ibid fo. 266)].

WILLIAM COOK.

The date of his institution to Lewisham is not known, but in 1396 he exchanged to Gingrave, in Essex, where he was admitted rector 9th June, 1396 (London Reg. 143 Bravbroke).

[A priest of this name was admitted rector of Widford, near Chelmsford (fo. 138 Braybroke), on 26th Jan., 1395, and resigned the same 1396].

JOHN KEYLMARSH

Had the King's licence to exchange South Mimms vicarage for the church of Birchanger, in Essex, with Robert de Wigorn, dated 1st Oct., 1351 (Pat. 25 Edw. III, p. 2).

On 1st Jan., 1355, he exchanged from Birchanger to the rectory of Radwinter with John de Arkesdon (Pat. 29 Edw. III, p. 3).

On 4th Kal. June, 1365, he was admitted vicar of Aldham, Essex (Lond. Reg., fo. 38 Sudbury), but resigned in 1370, apparently on being appointed to Bardfield Magna, Essex. This last he resigned in 1385 on exchanging to Abberton, Essex, with Henry Overdon, and was admitted to the rectory of Abberton 15th April, 1385 (Lond. Reg., fo. 35 Braybroke), but resigned the same year. He was then vicar of Cookham, in Berkshire, and exchanged in 1393 for the rectory of West Wickham, in Kent, but resigned shortly afterwards and was admitted rector of Gingrave, Essex, 3rd Sept., 1393 (Lond. Reg., fo. 114 Braybroke). This he held for three years and then exchanged with William Cock to Lewisham, where he was admitted vicar 6th June, 1396 ; patron, Richard II, by reason of the war with France (Reg. W. Bottlesham, fo. 82b). He was vicar of Lewisham until 1405, when he resigned, most probably from old age if the whole of the above appointments refer to the same man.

THOMAS OKEY,

Chaplain of the Gyldeaule, London, and chaplain of the perpetual chantry in the Church of St. James, Garlekhythe, for the souls of John Oxenford, Walter Nele and Sir John Denthorn. He was admitted vicar of Lewisham 27th Jan., 1405, on the resignation of John Keylmarsh (Reg. J. Bottlesham, fo. 190b).

RICHARD CHAPMAN

Was vicar in the reign of Henry V, c. 1420 ; according to Drake's Hasted he sought to recover his tithes by force (Chapt. Ho. 1. 1-22, 2).

WILLIAM FROME, LL.D.

Date of institution unknown. He was vicar on the 10th May, 1431, when an agreement was come to with the Prior of Shene, the patron, as to certain tithes (Reg. Spir. Roff. D., fo. 81a). He was elected Proctor for the Clergy in Convocation Oct., 1433 (Reg. Langdon, fo. 97b), and was vicar of Lewisham until 1441, when he exchanged to Chiddingfold, Surrey.

He exchanged Chiddingfold for the rectory of Long Ditton in 1448 (Reg. Wainflete I, fo. 9a), and was instituted there 21st Dec., 1448, and resigned the same in 1454 (ibid fo. 68b).

John Witton

Was vicar of Chiddingfold in 1426 (Manning and Bray's Surrey, vol. i, p. 655). This he resigned in 1441 and, exchanging with Dr. Frome, was admitted vicar of Lewisham 17th Nov., 1441 (Reg. W. Wellys, fo. 163). He died in June, 1444, and his will, dated 31st May, was proved 20th June of that year at Rochester (Book I, fo. 28b).

Peter Rickman.

He was admitted 3rd July, 1444, on the death of John Witton (Reg. J. Lowe, fo. 199b), and was vicar until 1459, when he resigned.

John Mallory

Was admitted vicar on 20th March, 1459, on the resignation of Peter Rykman ; patron, the Prior and Convent of Shene. (Register J. Lowe, fo. 233a). He was admitted also to the adjoining rectory of Lee on 10th Nov., 1462, on the presentation of Anthony Widville, Lord Scales (Reg. J. Lowe, fo. 237b), but this he resigned in 1463 (fo. 238a). He died July, 1467 (Act. Cur. Cons. 1443–1468, fo. 540a, 541a).

(A John Mallory, priest, was instituted to Ealing or Yealing vicarage, in London diocese, 24th Aug., 1437 (Lond. Reg. 8 Gilbert), and resigned in 1443 (fo. 51 Gilbert).

William Helwyse or Elwys

Was vicar in 1474 (mentioned in the will of John Crokker, Rochester Consistory Wills, Book IV, fo. 198), and also in 1484 (will of Roger Combe).

In 1478 "Dns. Wm. Holowys vicarius de Levesham" is witness to the will of Thomas Broke (Book VI, fo. 5).

On 21st April, 1478, Sir Wm. Elywys, vicar of Lewesham, witnessed the will of John Goldyng, smith (Book VI, fol. 7).

Roger Tochet, ll.b. & s.t.p.

He appears to have come to Lewisham before Helwyse left. He is mentioned as vicar in 1483 by Agnes Byllok in her will (Book VI, fo. 14a) and by Timothy Bates (Book VI, fo. 21a).

He was admitted to the rectory of St. Nicholas Coldeabby, London, on 4th Feb., 1492. He was also rector of Beckenham, but when appointed does not appear. He was rector there on 9th Sept., 1504 (Act. Vis. Archid., fo. 9a), also on 8th April, 1521 (will of John Fanaunt, Book VII, fo. 209b), and Oct. 17th, 1523 (Act. Vis. Archid., fo. 8b), and was taxed for the annual value thereof at £xx in 1523; also for the rectory of St. Nich. Coldabby, dio. Lond. (Lib. Tax., fo. 22a, 29a, 33b, 40b, 52a, 71b, 84a), and of Lewisham at £xix. He resigned Lewisham in 1530. He died in 1532, and his successor at Beckenham (Dr. Elizeus Bodley) was instituted 4th March, 1532.

(? Was Dr. Tochet of the family of Touchet, Baron Audley.)

JOHN CRAYFORD, D.D.

Instituted 5th July, 1530, on the resignation of Roger Tochet ; patron, the Prior and Convent of Shene (Reg. Spir. Roff. D., fo. 158b). He resigned in 1545.

He was elected a Fellow of Queen's College, Cambridge, in 1514, and of University College, Oxford, 1519 ; Canon of Cardinal College, Oxford, 1525 ; D.D. Cambridge, 1535, having in 1532 been appointed rector of Stamford Rivers, in Essex, but resigning the same was collated to Harleston Prebend in St. Paul's. He held also Prebends in St. Asaph, Westminster, and Winchester, and in 1544 was made chancellor of the church of Sarum, and in the following year collated to the Archdeaconry of Berks. In 1546 he was elected Master of University College, Oxford. He was rector of Newton Toney, Wilts, from 1545 until his death, in 1547.

Although he was vicar of Lewisham for fifteen years—1530 to 1545— there is no evidence of his having resided here. His curate, Sir William Bulkeley, signed the Papal Renunciation for him, as far as this living was concerned, in 1534.

In his will, dated 28th Aug., 1547, and proved 28th June, 1548 (P.C.C. 8 Populwell), he styles himself " Canon Resyden of the Cathedrall Church of Sarum," and speaks of his house in Warwyke Lane in London, the lease of which he left to " Mayster Doctor Anthonye Bellasses." He also left "a serpents tonge sett in golde " to the wife of Lord Wryothesley, Earl of Southampton. There are other similar bequests, but he does not mention Lewisham.

JOHN OLIVER, M.A.

Instituted 11th May, 1546, on the resignation of Dr. John Crayford; patron, Henry VIII (Register of Henry Holbeach, fo. 40a). He does not appear to have actually taken up his duties here, and nothing further is known of him.

JOHN GLYN

appears to have been in residence here—perhaps as curate—before his appointment as vicar. He witnessed the will of John Hodges, on 11th Oct., 1545 (Liber Test., XI, fo. 82b). He was presented to the living by Henry VIII in 1546 (Pat. 38 H viii, p. 1, m. 29), and was vicar here until his death in 1568. He was buried in the chancel on 28th Nov. in that year, and in his will left many charitable bequests to the poor of the parish, and £100 towards founding a school. He also mentions his house in London.

[A John Glyn, priest and curate of St. Anne's, Aldersgate, 1538, is mentioned in the will of Ingram Percy (P.C.C., Dingley); and a priest of the same name was admitted rector of St. Christopher's, London, 29th Jan., 1558 (fo. 480 Regr. Bonner, Bp. of London), but resigned in 1560 (Newcourt)].

It will be seen from the above that John Glyn was appointed to Lewisham in the reign of Henry VIII, and that he continued vicar without a break through the reigns of Edward VI and Mary, and died in 1568, well on in Elizabeth's reign, having seen the parish through that unsettled period. A full abstract of his will is given in the appendix to the Registers of St. Mary's, published by the Lewisham Antiquarian Society.

JOHN BUNGAY, M.A.,

Canon of Canterbury. Instituted 28th Nov, 1568, on the death of John Glyn; patron, Matthew Parker, Archbishop of Canterbury, for this turn (Reg. Episcopi, fo. 107a). He matriculated in 1553 at Corpus Christi College, Cambridge, and held several livings successively, among them Grantchester, Cambridgeshire, 1561; Lambeth, 1573; and Chartham. He does not seem to have spent much of his time at Lewisham, and was "presented" by the churchwardens on 3rd Sept., 1589, for non-residence. He died at Chartham, in Kent, 20th Nov., 1595, and was buried there. At the east end of the chancel of that church is a tablet to his memory with this inscription:—

"Here lieth y⁰ bodie of Mr. John Bungeye, clarke, one of y⁰ Prebendaries of Christ Churche in Cant. and Parson of this Parishe. Born in Norwich Jvly 7, A.D. 1536, whoe married Margaret Parker Borne in y⁰ same citie y⁰ 14 of Deceb. A.D. 1547, who lived together 35 years and had issue 8 sonns and 4 dvghtrs, which John bulded Mystole and there died ye 57 yeare of his age ye 20 of Noveb. A.D. 1595."

He was the first married vicar of Lewisham. His wife Margaret was daughter of Thomas Parker, the Archbishop's brother, and he was supervisor of that prelate's will.

ADRIAN DE SERAVIA, D.D.

Appointed 25th Nov., 1595, and instituted 15th March, 159⅚, on the death of Mr. Bungay.

He was born at Hedlin, in Artois, and studied for some time at Leyden University. He came to England about 1587, and was appointed rector of Tattenhall in Staffordshire in 1588. On 9th July, 1590, he was incorporated D.D. at Oxford. He was appointed canon of Canterbury, 6th Dec., 1595, and also of Westminster 5th July, 1601, and formed one of the committee appointed to translate the Bible. His episcopal ordination has been called in question ; but among his tracts is one on episcopacy, to which he ascribed a divine origin. Wood, in his " Fasti Oxonienses " (I, 252), says—" While he continued at Canterbury he had a just occasion given him to declare his judgment concerning episcopacy and sacrilege unto his brethren the ministers of the Low Countries, which was excepted against by Theodore Beza and others, against whose exceptions he rejoined and thereby became the happy author of several tracts in Latin, especially three, viz., ' De Diversis Ministrorum Evangelii Gradibus,' published in 1590."

These were translated and published in English in the following year, with the titles—

(1) " Of the Divers Degrees of the Ministers of the Gospel."
(2) "Of the Honour which is due unto Priests and Prelates of the Church."
(3) "Of Sacrilege and the Punishment thereof."

They were followed by one entitled "Concerning Christian Obedience to Princes."

His various writings were collected and printed in 1611, in one volume, by the Stationers' Company, and were reprinted by J. H. Parker, at Oxford, in 1840. Archdeacon Denison, in 1855, printed a translation of a tract by Dr. Seravia on the Holy Eucharist, with a notice of the author.

In 1610 he resigned the vicarage of Lewisham and went to Great Chart. He died 15th January, 16⅓, at Canterbury, aged 82, and was buried on the 19th of that month in the Cathedral Church, where there is a tablet to his memory by the north-west door of the nave, with this inscription :—

> Dilecto conivgi Hadriano de Seravia
> Margareta Wiits adhûc svperstes
> Qvacvm ille nuptias secundo iniit
> annosq. sex pie et feliciter vixit
> Memoriale hoc syncervm, Licet
> exigvvm Amoris svi qvasi pignvs
> ponendvm coravit.   Fvit is dvm vixit
> Theologiæ Doctor egregivs, Cathe-
> dralis hvius ecclesiæ Præbendarivs
> meritissimus, vir in omni literarvm
> Genere eximivs ; pietate, probitate,
> gravitate, svavitate, morvm Insignis :
> scriptis clarvs, Fide plenvs, et bonis
> operibus dives valde.   Natione Belga
> natvs Hedinæ Artesiæ.   Rexit
> Qvondam Lvgdvni Batavorvm Angliam
> Petit primo svb initivm Regni beatæ
> Memoriæ Elizabethæ.   Doctor
> (Lvgdvni ante creatvs) Oxoniæ
> Post incorporatvs est.
> In memoria æterna erit Ivstvs.
>   1612.

He married, firstly, Katherine Dallas, who died in 1605 and is buried in Canterbury Cathedral, and, secondly, Margaret Wiits, who survived him. She remarried on 1st June, 1614, at Canterbury Cathedral, the Rev. Robert Hill, D.D., rector of St. Bartholomew by the Exchange, London.

ABRAHAM COLFE, M.A.

Was the son of Richard Colfe, D.D., Prebendary of Canterbury, and was born in that city on 7th August, 1580, being baptized on the 14th idem at Holy Cross Church.   He was educated at the King's School and from thence passed to Christ Church College, Oxford, where he matriculated 8th Nov., 1594, and took his B.A. degree 25th Oct., 1599.   He was ad-mitted into Deacon's Orders 8th Jan., 1603, and Priest's 26th Feb., 1603 (Reg. Epi., fo. 199b).   He came to Lewisham at Michaelmas, 1604, as curate to Dr. Seravia, and was inducted vicar 1st May, 1610, on the presentation of his uncle, Joseph Colfe, Alderman of Canterbury, who had (apparently) obtained this turn from James I.

Mr. Colfe was vicar of Lewisham until his death on 5th Dec., 1657. Various attempts were made by the Puritan party to get him ejected from the living; but they were all unsuccessful, although he was obliged to resign the rectory of St. Leonard, Eastcheap, which he had held with Lewisham.

He married at Lee, on 3rd January, 16⅒, Margaret, daughter of John Holard, smith, and relict of Jasper Valentine, tanner, of Lewisham. She died in 1643, aged 79. His will, which has been printed and forms a quarto book of some 60 pages, provided, amongst numerous other matters, for the foundation of the Grammar School on Lewisham Hill and the Almshouses near the church.

He was buried in the churchyard, but his tomb is now covered by the church. There is a tablet to his memory on the exterior south wall, with this inscription :—" Here vnder lyeth bvried the body of Abraham Colf late minister of this Parish of Lewisham who departed this Life the fift day of Decemb. A° Dni. 1657."

A paper on "The Life and Times of Abraham Colfe," by Dr. Bramley, Head Master of Colfe's Grammar School, read before the Lewisham Antiquarian Society and subsequently printed, should be seen by those interested in this devoted pastor and his work for the good of the parish over which he presided at an especially try-ing juncture. Of his ministerial work we know little. In John Evelyn's diary are the following notes which refer to Mr. Colfe:—

"14 March, 1652, I went to Leusham, where I heard an honest sermon on 2 Corinth, 5, 7, being the first Sonday I had ben at Church since my returne, it being now a rare thing to find a priest of the Church of England in a parish pulpit, most of which were filld with Independents and Phanatics."

"25 Dec., 1652, Christmas Day, no sermon anywhere, no church being per-mitted to be open, so observ'd it at home. The next day we went to Lewesham where an honest divine preach'd."

[*Mr. John Bachiler* was appointed 26th Feb., 164½, as weekly lecturer, by the House of Commons. He and his friends complained to the House that he was much molested by Mr. Colfe, who in his will speaks of the wonderful unthank-fulness of some few of his parishioners, "when, at the instigation of their impudent Lecturer, they articled against me to the honorable Committee for plundered ministers, and endeavoured to have deprived me of my Vicarage."—Query : Was he the John Bachiler of Eman. Coll., Camb., author of "Golden Sand," &c., Lond. 1647 ; "The Virgins' Pattern," &c., Lond. 1661 ; and several sermons ?]

EDWARD TROTTER, M.A.

There was a note in the register, now burnt, that Mr. Trotter came to Lewisham on 26th July, 1658 ; but he was not instituted vicar until 3rd

Sept., 1660, when he was duly presented by Reginald Graham, Esq. (Reg. Spir. Roff. F, fo. 103b), and was inducted 7th Sept., 1660 (Reg. Elizei Burges, fo. 251a).

He died on 6th Sept., 1677, and was buried in the chancel, near Mr. Glyn, on 10th idem. There is a tablet to his memory on the exterior of the south wall of the church, with this inscription :—

"Near this place lies the body of the Rev. Edward Trotter, the fifth Vicar of this Parish after the Reformation, who died 6th Sept., 1677, aged 74 years.

"Also Capt. John Trotter, son of the above Rev. Edward Trotter, who died 12th Nov., 1747, aged 72 years.

"Also William, son of the above Capt. John Trotter, who died 19th Nov., 1809, aged 77 years."

ALEXANDER DAVISON, M.A.

He was the son of the Rev. Alexander Davison, M.A., vicar of Norham-on-Tweed, who, after being ejected from Norham by the Puritans, was reinstated at the Restoration. Mr. Davison was admitted into Deacon's Orders 23rd Sept., 1671, and was instituted to the rectory of Ford, in Northumberland, in 1676. On 2nd March, 1677, he was instituted vicar of Lewisham upon the death of Mr. Trotter, at the presentation of Reginald Graham, Esq., and Susanna, his wife, and held both livings until his death, July, 1689. He was buried at Norham-on-Tweed on the 10th of that month, probably beside his father, who had died in the February preceding. There was a note in the registers, now lost, that he was brother-in-law to Edward Trotter, his predecessor.

GEORGE STANHOPE, D.D., Dean of Canterbury.

Instituted vicar 3rd August, 1689, on the death of Mr. Davison, on the presentation of George, Baron Dartmouth, to whom he had been chaplain.

He was born at Hertishorn, in Derbyshire, 5th March, 16⅗⅘, his father, the Rev. Thos. Stanhope, being rector of that place, and from Uppingham School he passed to Eton and thence to King's College, Cambridge. He took B.A., 1681, and M.A., 1685, and was minister of Quoi, near Cambridge, and vice-Proctor in 1688, and was that year preferred to the rectory of Tring, in Hertfordshire. He was successively chaplain to King William and Queen Mary and Queen Anne. He took his Doctor's degree in 1697, and became vicar of Deptford in 1703, having previously been appointed to Lewisham as stated above. In 1703 he succeeded Dr.

Hooper as Dean of Canterbury, and was thrice Prolocutor of the Lower House of Convocation. He died 18th March, 172⅝, aged 68, and was buried in the chancel at Lewisham.

He was a somewhat voluminous writer. Amongst his works is a Paraphrase and Comment upon the Epistles and Gospels, in 4 vols., and a Book of Private Prayers for every day in the week and for the several parts of each day, translated out of the Greek Devotions of Bishop Andrews, which ran through several editions.

He is said to have been master of Latin, Greek, Hebrew and French, and his pulpit oratory to have been of a high order. Amongst his published sermons is one on Deut. xxxiii, 29, preached before the Queen at St. Paul's, 27th June, 1706, being the day appointed for a general thanksgiving for the success of Her Majesty's arms in Flanders and Spain.

Dr. Stanhope married, firstly, Olivia, daughter of Charles Cotton, Esq., of Beresford in Staffordshire, by whom he had one son, George, and five daughters, Catherine, Mary, Jane, Elizabeth and Charlotte. She died 1st June, 1707. He married, secondly, Ann, sister of Sir Charles Wager, who died 1st Oct., 1730, aged 54.

A full abstract of his will is given in the Appendix to the Lewisham Registers, printed in 1891.

The vicarage-house was rebuilt by Dr. Stanhope in 169⅔.

A monument—now on the wall under the northern gallery—was erected to his memory, with the following inscription :—

In memory
of the very Rev⁴ George Stanhope D.D.
38 years Vicar of this Parish and 26 of
the neighbouring Church of Deptford
Dean of Canterbury A.D. 1703
and thrice Prolocutor of the Lower House
of Convocation.
Whose piety was real and rational
his charity great and universal
Fruitful in acts of mercy and in all good works.
His learning was elegant and comprehensive
his conversation polite and delicate.
Grave without Preciseness, Facetious without Levity
The good Christian and solid Divine
and the fine gentleman
in him were happily united.
Who, tho' amply qualified for the Highest
Honours of his Sacred Function
yet was content with only Deserving them
In his Pastoral office a pattern to his people
And to all who shall succeed him in yᵉ care of them.

His Discourses from the Pulpit
were equally pleasing and profitable
a beautiful intermixture of ye clearest Reasoning
with ye purest Diction
attended with all the Graces of just Elocution
As his works from ye Press have spoke ye Praises
of his happy Genius, his love of God and man
for which Generations to come
will bless his Memory
He was born March y^e 5
He died March y^e 18, 1727
aged 68 years.

JOHN INGLIS, M.A.

Instituted 3rd April, 1728, on the death of Dr. Stanhope; patron, William, Earl of Dartmouth. He was a son of Alexander Inglis, of Salisbury, Wilts, gent., and matriculated 27th Feb., 171$\frac{9}{7}$, aged 17 ; graduated B.A., Christ Church, Oxon, 13th Oct., 1720; M.A., 21st June, 1723 (Foster's Alumni Oxonienses).

He died 18th October, 1739, and was buried in Lewisham churchyard (not at Chelsea as is sometimes stated) on the 27th idem, where there was this inscription to him :—

" Here lieth interred the body of the Rev. Mr. John Inglis, 11 years and 7 months vicar of this parish, who departed this life 18th October, 1739, aged 40.

"Also the body of Mr. John Inglis, M.D., uncle of the above, Fellow of the Royal Society, Assistant Master and Marshell of the Ceremonies in the Reigns of Queen Anne, King George the 1st and his present Majesty, who departed this life viii May, MDCCXL, aged 77.

"Also the body of Catherine, wife of the above Rev. John Inglis, by whom he had xiv children, who departed this life 17th June, 1747, aged 41."

This tomb still remains on the north side of the churchyard, near the yard wall, but the inscriptions have unfortunately been removed.

WILLIAM LOWTH, M.A.

Inducted 7th Dec., 1739, on the death of Mr. Inglis; patron, William, Earl of Dartmouth.

He was son of the Rev. Wm. Lowth, B.D., Prebendary of Winchester, by his wife Margaret Pitt. Matriculated 13th May, 1724, aged 17, Magdalen College, Oxford ; B.A., 5th Feb., 172$\frac{7}{8}$; M.A., 13th Nov., 1730. (Foster's Alumni Oxon.) He was appointed vicar of St. Margaret's, Rochester,

1731, and of Lewisham 1739, and a Prebendary of Winchester 1759. His brother, Robert, was Bishop of London.

Mr. Lowth's neice, Mary Eden, married Ebenezer Blackwell, of The Limes, Lewisham, the friend of John Wesley, and he must have seen much of the great preacher during his visits to the Blackwells. We are entitled to assume that this combination of circumstances prevented the religious life of the parish from falling as low as it did in some places during the last century. Wesley used frequently to preach at Lewisham, on one occasion, at least, in the parish church ; and Mr. Blackwell was one of the foremost in helping to carry out the rebuilding of St. Mary's in 1774-77.

Mr. Lowth died in 1795, and was buried in the churchyard, close to the Blackwell obelisk. His tomb has this inscription :—

" Here lieth the body of the Rev. William Lowth M.A. 55 years Vicar of this Parish who died April the 30, 1795.

" Here lieth the body of Mrs. Elizabeth Lowth wife of the Rev. William Lowth Vicar of this Parish, who died Aug. 25, 1765."

HUGH JONES, M.A.

Instituted 22nd Aug., 1795, on the death of Mr. Lowth. He was son of Mr. Roger Jones, of Llanrhydd, Co. Denbigh. He matriculated 3rd March, 1767, aged 17, Queen's College, Oxford ; B.A., 10th Oct., 1770 ; M.A., 17th Dec., 1773. (Foster's Alumni Oxon.)

He appears from the registers to have come to Lewisham in 1789 as curate to Mr. Lowth, and on the latter's death, in 1795, he was presented to the living, which, however, he resigned in favour of the Hon. Edward Legge in 1797. He continued to act as curate until 1825, when he was re-appointed vicar, having in the meantime held the rectory of Talgarth, Brecon, to which he was presented in 1806.

He was, previous to his coming to Lewisham, curate of Southfleet, Kent, and, whilst there, married Jane Swift, of Northfleet, on 29th Dec., 1784. She died 27th January, 1828, having had issue two daughters, Maria and Charlotte, born at Northfleet in 1787 and 1789, and two sons, Thomas Swift Jones, born at the vicarage-house, Lewisham, 2nd Oct., 1791, and Edward Lewis Jones, also born at the vicarage, 16th July, 1795, " just after his Father's induction into the Living of Lewisham " (entry in the family Bible).

HON. EDWARD LEGGE, D.C.L., Bishop of Oxford.

Instituted 1797, on the resignation of Mr. Jones. He was the seventh son of William, second Earl of Dartmouth. Born 4th Dec., 1767, and educated at Rugby. Matriculated 14th June, 1784, Christ Church, Oxford ; B.A., 11th April, 1788; Fellow of All Souls' College, 1789; B.C.L., 9th June, 1791 ; D.C.L., 6th April, 1805 ; Warden, 1817–1827, having been appointed a Prebendary of Winchester 1795 and vicar of Lewisham in 1797, and in the same year a Prebendary of Canterbury. In 1802 he was appointed a Canon of Windsor, and further advanced to the Deanery in 1805. In 1815 the King nominated him to the Bishopric of Oxford, which he held until his death on 27th Jan., 1827. He continued to hold the vicarage of Lewisham until 1825, and his signature from time to time in the parish books shows that he was not neglectful of his parishioners.

HUGH JONES, M.A.,

Re-appointed 19th March, 1825, on the resignation of the Bishop of Oxford.

He died at the vicarage-house 3rd July, 1831, aged 79, and was buried at Lewisham on the 8th of that month. There is no monument to his memory.

HON. HENRY LEGGE, D.C.L.

Instituted 11th Aug., 1831, on the death of Mr. Jones. He was the fifth son of George, third Earl of Dartmouth, born 25th Sept., 1805, and educated at Eton. He matriculated 22nd Jan., 1822, Christ Church, Oxford ; B.A., 13th May, 1825 ; Fellow of All Souls' College, 1825-42 ; B.C.L. 26th March, 1835 ; D.C.L., 26th March, 1840.

He took Orders in 1826, and was curate to the Hon. and Rev. George Neville (afterwards Dean of Windsor) at Hawarden, in Flintshire, from 1827 to 1831. He was appointed vicar of Lewisham, as above, in 1831, and held the living until 1879, when he resigned on account of failing health.

He died 13th Feb., 1887, and is buried in Lewisham Cemetery.

He married, in 1842, Marian, daughter of Sir Frederick Leman Rogers, Bart., of Blachford, Devonshire, but left no issue.

HON. AUGUSTUS LEGGE, D.D.

Instituted Oct., 1879, on the resignation of the Hon. Henry Legge. He is the fifth son of William Walter, late Earl of Dartmouth ; born 28th Nov., 1839; educated at Eton. He matriculated 21st Oct., 1857, Christ Church, Oxford ; B.A., 1861 ; M.A., 1864 ; D.D., 1891 ; admitted to Deacon's Orders Sept., 1864 ; Priest's, 1865. Curate of Handsworth, Birmingham, 1864, and St. Mary's, Bryanston Square, 1866, and vicar of St. Bartholomew's, Sydenham, 1867, which last he resigned on being appointed to Lewisham in 1879. He was subsequently Honorary Canon of Rochester, Proctor in Convocation, and Rural Dean of Lewisham. During his vicariate the interior of the nave of the parish church was remodelled and a chancel added, while the parochial institutions were re-arranged to meet the requirements of a district which had grown from a country village into a populous suburb of London.

In the summer of 1891 he was nominated to the Bishopric of Lichfield, being consecrated on Michaelmas Day, and consequently resigned the vicarage of Lewisham.

Dr. Legge married, 3rd June, 1877, Fanny Louisa, 2nd daughter of William Bruce Stopford-Sackville, Esq., and has issue two sons and two daughters.

SAMUEL BICKERSTETH, M.A.

Instituted 30th Nov., 1891, on the resignation of Dr. Legge ; patron, the Crown for this turn. He is second son of Edward Henry [Bickersteth], Bishop of Exeter, and was born 9th Sept., 1857. Matriculated St. John's College, Oxford, 14th Oct., 1876; B.A., 1881; M.A., 1883. Curate of Christ Church, Lancaster Gate, 1881 to 1884, and private chaplain to Dr. Boyd Carpenter, Bishop of Ripon, 1884 to 1887. In 1887 he was presented to the vicarage of All Saints', Belvedere, Kent, and preferred to that of Lewisham as stated above.

He married 21st June, 1881, Ella Chlora Faithfull, daughter of Sir Monier Monier-Williams, K.C.I.E., D.C.L., Boden Professor of Sanskrit in the University of Oxford, and has issue five sons.

Curates.

The names of the curates from 1497 to 1600 are mostly obtained from the wills of parishioners to which they appear as witnesses. The references are to the Will Registers of the Consistory Court of Rochester, unless otherwise stated. Before the early registers were destroyed a list of curates and vicars named therein was extracted and is with the parish papers ; this will explain the reference against Thos. Bullock, Thos. Percyvall, &c.

From 1700 the names have been obtained from the Registers, and details gleaned from Foster's Alumni Oxonienses, Cambridge University Lists, Crockford's Clerical Directory, &c.

1497 | SIR RICHARD OVERYE, curate,
1498 | Is witness to the will of Richard Gryme, of Sepnam, 1497 ; and of
              John a Bery, of Leuysham, 1498 (Book V, folios 319 and 341).

1498   SIR JOHN MALYN, parish priest,
              Is mentioned in the will of Robert Cheseman, gent., dated 18th
              March, 1498 (P.C.C. 20 Horne).

1502   SIR LEWAS YALE, curate,
              Witnessed the will of Thos. Owterede, tanner, 1502 (VI, 53).

1504   SIR THOMAS RUSSELL, parish priest,
              Witnessed the will of Wm. Grenrygge, dated 15th Feb., 1504 (P.C.C.
              26 Holgrave).

1509 | SIR JOHN ASCHELY, curate,
1513 | First appears as witness to the will of John Smyth, on 9th Sept., 1509
              (VI, 256). He died in 1513, and his will was proved that year
              on 26th Oct. (VI, 367). The following is a verbatim copy
              thereof. It is of interest as a specimen of wills of the period :—
            Dᵐ Johes Aschley, curatus de Leuysham.
              In the name of God Amen the v daie of Sept. in the yere of
              our lorde mˡ vᶜ xiij I Sir John Aschley of Leuysh'm p'ste
              make my testament in this wise Furste I bequeth my soull to
              God my bodie to be buried be fore our ladie in the chaunsell
              of Lewish'm Churche. Itm. I bequeith to the makeyng of a
              pixe in the saide churche a Rynge of golde. Itm. I gif to the
              saide church a sirpless wt a sachell to putt it in. Itm. I

bequeth to the Rep'acion of the saide churche x^s I bequeith
to Sir William Branlyng a gown of tauney that I made last, he
to synge for my soull xiij masses at Scala cele.   Itm. I gif to
Sr John Watkynson a boke callid Vitas Patrum.   Itm. I gif to
my brother Nicholas Aschley a spone w^t a knopp silu^r.   Itm.
I will my executo's schall reward hym sumwhate as schall
please them.   Itm. I will that myn executours schall spende at
my burying xl^s And the residue of my goodes I bequeith to
myn executours whom I make Mr John Cheseman and Ric.
Wyncham.   Witnes Sr William Branlyng and Henry Johnson.

1514   SIR THOMAS CLARKE, curate,
    Witnessed the will of John Kichell, dated 14th June, 1514
    (VII, 18).

1514   SIR JOHN PARKER, curate,
    Was a witness to the will of Thomas Reede, yeoman, dated 3rd Dec.,
    1514 (VII, 27).

1515   SIR CHRISTOFER FAUKNER, curate,
    Witness to the will of John Batt, on 8th March, 1515 (VII, 56).

1517   SIR WILLIAM HEWET, curate,
    Witnessed the will of John Fraunces, on 14th Jan., 1517 (VII, 112).

1520 }   SIR WILLIAM BULKELEY, curate.
1534 }   He first appears as a witness to the will of Stephen Levendale, on
    10th April, 1520 (VII, 187).   He witnessed wills in 1521 and
    1522, and that of Adam Momforth, on 14th April, 1523 (ibid,
    268), and of Jone Johnson, widow, on 15th Oct., 1532 (IX, 49).
    In 1534 he signed the renunciation of the Papal authority for
    the vicar of Lewisham (Dr. John Crayford).

1524 }   SIR THOMAS WADE, curate,
1532 }   Witnessed the will of Thomas Johnson, on 22nd Nov., 1524 (VII,
    353); of William Berepikle, on 3rd April, 1527 (VIII, 118); of
    Stephen Kynge, on 6th June, 1531 (IX, 12); and of Alexander
    Blake, 14th March, 1532 (IX, 34).

1534 }
1538 }   SIR JOHN COPLAND, curate,

A witness to the will of Robert Batt, on 23rd Jan., 1534 (IX, 265), and to that of John Hankin, 28th Feb., 1538 (IX, 265).

1541   SIR JOHN TOWNE, curate,

Witnessed the will of Owyne Doddesworthe, on 10th March, 1541 (IX, 340).

1542 }
1543 }   JOHN HALE, curate,

Witnessed the will of Walter Batt, on 6th May, 1542 (X, 390), and that of John Rede, on 16th Nov., 1543 (X, 40).

1545   HENRY MANNERING, clarke,

Witnessed the will of Steven Bat, 30th Nov., 1545 (ibid, 140).

1545 }
1548 }   SIR MILES NORTH, curate,

Was a witness to the will of John Holande, on 12th April, 1545 (fo. 161), and of John Chibnoll, 12th Aug., 1546 (fo. 193). He was chantry priest of Richard Walker's chantry, in the chapel of the Holy Trinity in Lewisham Church, at its suppression in 1548.

1546   SIR LEWES TOMLYN

Witnessed the will of Henry Bat, on 13th March, 1546 (ibid, 196).

1545 }
1546 }   SIR MARTYN LYSTER, curate,

His will was proved on 6th October, 1546; it is as follows: In the name of God, Amen. The ixth day of nouember in the yere of o^r lord God m^{l}v^{c}xlvth I Martyn Lyster clarke and also curate at Lewsham beyng p'fite of mynd make this my last will after man^r and forme followyng. First and principallie I do gyue and bequeythe my soule to Almightye God and my body to be buryed in the Church yarde of Lewsham afforesaid. Also I gyue and bequeythe vnto my brother Xpo^r Lyster the deds of the lands that lyeth in Hempsingham for in my coustyaunce the Right and Tytill lyeth and is onllie in lying. The which deds ar in my Cooffer in a whyte cappe. Also I will vnto my said brother Xpo^r Lyster vj^{li} xiij^s iiij^d to be payed of myn execut^r when

he gettethe the money that is dewe vnto me for the lease of
Temys Dytty. Itm. I bequeythe to the p'son of Saynt Martins
in the vyntre my best Clooke. I gyue and bequeythe vnto
Maryon Thomson my secound Coote and all my gere about my
body y' is app'ell at my dep'tyng. Also I will y' myn execut' do
pay rent for the same Maryon for one half yere. Also I do gyue
and bequeythe vnto S' John Scotte my long blewe gown, a payre
of Hoose, a payre of Shoes and a cappe. The Resydue of my
goods moveable and vnmoveable I do gyue and bequeythe vnto
James Jankynson whome I make my full executo' and he to se
me honestlie buryed and my debts payed. Theis Wytnesses
Edward Saunder, prest, Robert Hayle parson of Lee, and John
Cossyn with other (X, 184).

1555 }
1558 } NICHOLAS (or RICHARD) MEDCALF, curate,
    Mentioned by Julyan Granger, widow, in her will dated 1555
    (XII, 350).

1560 }
1563 } RICHARD SKINNER, priest,
    Witnessed the will of Thomas Hunt on 7th June, 1563 (XIII, 13).

1567 SIR WILLIAM HEWET, clerk,
    Witnessed the wills of Robert Comforte of Sypnam, 1567 (XIII,
    330), and John Levendale, 19th May, 1567 (fo. 336).

1570 }
1574 } WILLIAM WALTON, curate,
    Mentioned in the will of Richard Gryme, 1570 (XIII, 464), and
    witnessed the will of John Kenworth, 7th Dec., 1574 (P.C.C. 1,
    Pickering).

1576 JOHN PARCELL, curate,
    Witness, with John Hall, "one of the sidmen," to the will of
    Christofer Gardnett, tanner, 1576 (XV, 24).

1577 }
1578 } THOMAS BULLOCK, curate.
    His name was in the register (now burnt) in 1577, and on 6th Oct.,
    1578, he witnessed the will of Richard Davies (XVI, 48).

1581 }
1583 } WILLIAM REDMAN, curate,
    Witness to the will of John Currie, yeoman, on 28th April, 1581
    (XVI, 233). He was buried at Lewisham on 9th February,

1583, with his daughter Catherine.   In the register he is styled
"Clerk and minister of God's Word."

1584   THOMAS PERCYVALL.

His name, as curate, occurred in the registers for 1584.

1589 }   RICHARD LIGHTFOOT, minister,
1593 }   Witnessed the will of Henry Bateman, 25th Feb., 1589 (XVIII, 56),
            and of John Greate, yeoman, 25th Jan., 159⅜ (ibid, 216).   He
            was curate of St. Lawrence Poultney in 1598 (Newcourt I, 918).

1594 }   JOHN WORSHIP.
1596 }   His name, as curate, was in the registers (now burnt) for 1594.   On
            27th June, 1596, he witnessed the will of Madlyne Dawborne,
            widow, and on 4th Nov., 1596, that of William Johnson
            (XVIII, 515 & 611.   [A John Worship, priest, was instituted
            1st July, 1598, to the Rectory of Grinsted next Colchester, on
            the presentation of Queen Elizabeth (Grindall, 304), but resigned
            the same year (Newcourt II, 287)].

1599   JAMES FOWRESTIER.

His name was in the register for 1599.

1603   FRANCIS DEE, M.A.

His name occurred, in the register (now burnt) for 1603, as curate to
Dr. Hadrian de Semvia.   He was son of David Dee, of Salop
(said to have been rector of St. Bartholomew's, Smithfield), by
Martia, daughter of John Rogers, and was educated at Merchant
Taylors' School; Fellow of St. John's College, Cambridge,
1596; M.A., 1603; B.D., 1610; D.D., 1617.   From Lewisham
he went to London and was rector of Trinity the Less, 1606,
and of Alhallows, Lombard Street, 1615; Chancellor of Salisbury, 1619; vicar of Sutton in Kent, 1621; Dean of Chichester,
1630; rector of Castor, Northants, 1634; and finally Bishop of
Peterborough, 1634 until his death 8th Oct., 1638.   He was
buried in the choir of the Cathedral Church.

He married, firstly, Susan, daughter of Nicholas le Porcque,
by whom he had :—

1. Adrian Dee, M.A., only son—named apparently after his
   former vicar at Lewisham—born 1st Dec., 1607; entered

Merchant Taylors' School 27th March, 1620; Canon
residen. of Chichester, 1633; and died, unmarried, 8th
May, 1638.

2. Mary, only daughter, married twice, but left no issue. She
died 17th Dec., 1670, aged 63.

He married, secondly, Elizabeth, daughter of Rev. Jn. Winter,
Preb. of Canterbury, by whom he had no children. (See Wilson's
History of Merchant Taylors' School, vol. ii.)

1604 } ABRAHAM COLFE, M.A.,
1610 }   Afterwards vicar until his death, 1657.

1656   WILLIAM RICHARDSON,
             Curate to Mr. Colfe, and mentioned in his will dated 1656.

1678   GEORGE BALL,
             Chaplain to the Earl of Carlisle, was curate to Mr. Davidson.

1679 } MICHAEL QUEENBURGE
1683 }   Succeeded Mr. Ball as curate to Mr. Davison. He witnessed the
             will of Matthew Delver, on 6th Dec., 1679 (XXV, 412). A note
             in the register stated that he went away 16th January, 1683.

             [A Michael Quinbrough, son of William Quinbrough of
             Coventry, occurs in Foster's Alumni Oxon. as matriculating at
             Oxford, 11th May, 1670, aged 18 (St. Mary Hall); and as vicar
             of Exhall, Warwickshire, 1686.]

1694   ROBERT ORM, curate,
             Had a child buried in 1694, and another in 1699. In 1703 two
             children of " Mr. Orm's, from London, once curate here," were
             buried; and he himself was buried here, from London, on 17th
             January, 173¾.

1705 } JOHN CLENDON, M.A.
1709 }   Mentioned in the registers, and by Dr. Stanhope, in his Diary of
             Accounts.

             He was son of John Clendon, of Handen, Northamptonshire,
             gent. Magdalen Hall, Oxon., matriculated 17th April, 1693,
             aged 16; B.A., 1696; M.A., 1699; of the Inner Temple, 1691.
             Rector of Harleston, Northants, 1710 until his death. He was
             buried there 25th April, 1756. (Foster's Alumni Oxon.)

1712, &c. BENJAMIN WORSTER,

>Emanuel College, Cambridge. B.A., 1704 ; M.A., 1708.

>[A Ben. Worster is witness to the will of Timothy Clarke, 21st Dec., 1712 (XXX, 10.)]

>Dr. Stanhope has entries of payments to "Mr. Worster" in his Diary of Accounts.

1718, &c. —— ARCHER.

>Dr. Stanhope mentions " Mr. Archer" as serving the cure in 1718 and other years.

1720 }
1754 }   ABRAHAM HECKSTALL,

>Jesus Coll., Camb. B.A., 1717 ; M.A., 1722. His son Edward was baptized at Lewisham 21st July, 1725, and buried 16th Sept., 1726. His wife was buried 20th May, 1730, and his daughter, " Mrs. Philipie," on 16th Jan., 173⅜. He died on 28th March, 1754, aged 61, and was buried in the churchyard, where there is a stone to his memory and that of his son, the Rev. Brooke Heckstall, LL.D. (Emmanuel Coll. Camb.), rector of St. Ann, Aldersgate, who died 5th April, 1780, aged 55.

1752   BARTHOLOMEW SABOURN,

>"Master of Mr. Colfe's English School, reader of Blackheath Chapel and Assistant Curate to yᵉ Vicar of Lewisham," was buried 9th Oct., 1752.

1750 }
1761 }   GEORGE DOWNING.

>[A George Downing, son of Dickson Downing of Denmark Hill, London, gent., matriculated Wadham Coll., Oxon., 18th May, 1745, aged 16 ; B.A., 11th Feb., 174⅚ ; M.A., 1751. (Foster's Alumni Oxon.)]

1761   JOHN DEERE THOMAS,

>Son of Evan Thomas, of Clerkenwell, gent. Jesus College, Oxford, matriculated 27th March, 1754, aged 18 ; B.A., 1757 ; M.A., 1760 ; B. and D.D., 1786 ; rector of Kirby Misperton, Yorkshire, 1780 until his death in 1819. (Foster's Alumni Oxon.)

1762–72 W. BUDWORTH.

1772–78 JOHN LEVETT or LIVETT.

1778–89 JOSHUA MORTON.

1789 } HUGH JONES, M.A.
1825 }   He was afterwards vicar.

1819–49 EVAN MORGAN.

1825   WM. TILDEN.
     [A William Tilden at Sidney Sussex Coll., Camb., B.A., 1823.]

1829 } JOHN SATTERTHWAITE HANSON WELSH,
1849 }   Eldest son of John Welsh, of St. George's, Hanover Square, London,
     gent. Queen's College, Oxford, matriculated 17th January, 1820,
     aged 19; B.A., 1825; M.A., 1826. He died 26th October,
     1855. (Foster's Alumni Oxon.)

1827   R. T. LANCASTER.
     [See Foster's Alumni Oxonienses—A Richard Thomas Lancaster,
     son of Rev. Richard Hume Lancaster, of St. Pancras, London,
     Exeter Coll., Oxon., matriculated 4th July, 1815, aged 16; B.A.,
     1819; M.A., 1825. Afterwards resided at Brighton and Chel-
     tenham, and died 24th Dec., 1882.]

1849 } JOHN MICHELL CLARKE.
1854 }   St. John's College, Cambridge, B.A., 1846; M.A., 1850. He was
     curate of Dethick, Derbyshire, 1847-49; then at Lewisham from
     1849 to 1854, when he was appointed vicar of Christ Church,
     Forest Hill. In 1878 he was presented to the rectory of Fenny
     Drayton, Leicestershire.

1854 } GEORGE PHILIP OTTEY.
1863 }   St. John's College, Cambridge, B.A., 1847; M.A., 1871. Prebendary
     of St. Paul's, 1876; Inspector of Schools in the Diocese of
     London, 1871; rector of Much Hadham, Hertfordshire, 1886
     to 1889. He died in 1891.

1863 ⎱ WALTER JAMES SOWERBY.
1869 ⎰
　　　　St. John's College, Cambridge, B.A., 1855; M.A., 1858. Curate of
　　　　Moulsham, Essex, 1856-59; of Romford, 1859-63, when he
　　　　came to Lewisham. In 1869 he was presented to the vicarage
　　　　of Eltham.

1858 ⎱ ROBERT HALL,
1869 ⎰
　　　　Son of James Hall, Esq., of Kingsholm, Gloucester. Scholar of
　　　　Christ's College, Cambridge; matriculated Oct., 1846; B.A.,
　　　　1850; M.A., 1854. Curate of Strood, Kent, 1855 to 1858.
　　　　From Lewisham he went to Maisemore, Gloucestershire. In
　　　　1873 he was presented to the vicarage of Gorsley, in the same
　　　　county, and in 1876 to Flaxley, and finally to that of Saul in
　　　　1883.

1870 ⎱ WILLIAM HANSON JACKSON,
1879 ⎰
　　　　Son of the Rev. John Jackson, of Butterwick, Lincolnshire. Clare
　　　　College, Cambridge, matriculated Oct., 1861; B.A., 1864;
　　　　M.A., 1873. Curate of Yaxley, Hunts, 1866 to 1869; and of
　　　　Croyland, 1869-70. He was curate of Lewisham from 1870 to
　　　　1879, the latter part of the time in charge. From 1879 to 1881
　　　　he was in charge of St. Paul's, Deptford, and in the latter year
　　　　he was presented by the Bishop of the Diocese to the vicarage
　　　　of Frindsbury, near Rochester.

1879 ⎱ MUIRHEAD MITCHELL CONNOR.
1882 ⎰
　　　　Christ's College, Cambridge, B.A., 1875; M.A., 1880. He was
　　　　presented to the vicarage of West Bromwich, Staffordshire, 1882.
　　　　Chaplain to the Bishop of Lichfield, 1891.

1879 ⎱ CHARLES MORTIMER McANALLY,
1880 ⎰
　　　　Son of the Rev. David McAnally. Magdalene College, Cambridge,
　　　　B.A., 1877; M.A., 1880. From Lewisham he went to St.
　　　　Jude's, South Kensington, and in 1888 was presented to the
　　　　vicarage of St. James', Hampstead.

1880 ⎱ CHARLES HARE SIMPKINSON.
1881 ⎰
　　　　Son of Rev. John Nassau Simpkinson, M.A., rector of North Creake,
　　　　Norfolk. Balliol College, Oxford, matriculated Jan., 1874;
　　　　B.A., 1877; M.A., 1881. Vicar of Holy Trinity, Blackheath

Hill, 1881-7, and of St. Paul's, Lorrimore Square, Walworth, 1887. Examining Chaplain to the Bishop of Winchester, 1891.

1881 }
1886 } CHARLES DRUCE FARRAR.

King's College, London, 1879, and B.A., Durham, 1881. Curate of St. Margaret's, Lee, 1880-81. In 1886-7 he was Inspector of Schools, Diocese of London. In the latter year he was presented to the vicarage of Micklefield, Yorkshire.

1886 }
1891 } CHARLES JASPER PALMER.

Son of the Rev. G. T. Palmer, M.A., rector of St. Mary, Newington, Surrey. Pembroke College, Cambridge, B.A., 1889. In 1891 he was appointed Chaplain of St. Paul's Cathedral, Calcutta.

1886 }
1891 } TOM HORATIO FOSTER.

Eldest son of Williamson Foster, Esq., of Leeds, Yorkshire. Exeter College, Oxford, B.A., 1886. In 1891 he was appointed Domestic Chaplain to the Bishop of Lichfield.

1883 }
1888 } WILLIAM HOOK LONGSDON.

Son of the Rev. Henry John Longsdon, M.A., sometime rector of Keighley, Yorkshire. He matriculated 10th Oct., 1878, Trinity College, Cambridge; B.A., Jan., 1882; M.A., April, 1885. Curate of St. Mary's, Lewisham, Dec., 1883, to Dec., 1888, when he became curate of St. Laurence's, Catford. He was assistant master in Colfe's Grammar School, Lewisham, 1882-90.

1883 }
1886 } FRANCIS HENRY PAYNE-GALLWEY.

Son of Philip Payne-Gallwey, Esq., of Brafferton Moor, Yorkshire. Trinity College, Cambridge, B.A., 1882. He was curate of St. Mary's from Dec., 1883, to June, 1886, when he was presented to the rectory of Kirkby-Knowle, Yorkshire.

1889 }
1891 } RICHARD POLGREEN ROSEVEARE.

Son of William Roseveare, Esq., of Monmouth. St. John's College, Cambridge, B.A., 1888. Curate of St. Mary's, 1889 to 1891, and assistant master in St. Dunstan's College, Catford. Early in 1892 he was appointed curate of Fenton, Staffordshire, and later to the charge of the district of Danby Main, in the parish of Mexborough and Conisborough, Yorkshire.

1890 } HAROLD ATHELSTONE PARRY SAWYER
1891 }
    Son of the Right Rev. William Collinson Sawyer, first Bishop of
Grafton and Armidale, New South Wales. Matriculated, 1883,
Queen's College, Oxford; B.A., 1887; M.A., 1892. Curate of
St. Mary's, 1890 to 1891, and assistant master in St. Dunstan's
College, Catford. In 1892 he was appointed assistant master in
Highgate College.

1891   THOMAS BEEDHAM CHARLESWORTH.
    Son of Charles Henry Charlesworth, Esq., of Holly Bank, Settle,
Yorkshire. Matriculated, Oct., 1885, Christ's College, Cambridge; B.A., 1888; M.A., 1892. Assistant master in Worces-
ter Grammar School, 1888-89. Appointed curate of St. Mary's,
Lewisham, 1891.

1891   THOMAS EDMUND TEIGNMOUTH SHORE.
    Son of Rev. Thomas Teignmouth Shore, Canon of Worcester.
Matriculated, 21st Oct., 1886, Magdalen College, Oxford; B.A.,
1890. Appointed curate of St. Mary's, 1891.

₊ This list does not include the names of those who of late years, although
licensed to St. Mary's, have had charge of the chapel in Dartmouth
Row, Blackheath (now the Church of the Ascension), or the chapelry of
Southend.

ADDENDA.

The following were inadvertently omitted from page 65 :-

1882 | EDWARD CECIL ROBINSON.
1888 /   Son of Charles Backhouse Robinson, Esq., of Frankton Grange,
Salop, formerly of Liverpool. Matriculated 8th Dec., 1868,
Exeter College, Oxford; B.A., 1872; M.A., 1876. He was
curate of Christ Church, Lichfield, 1873 to 1876; of St. Mary's,
Woolwich, 1876 to 1879; and of St. Michael's, Lower Sydenham, 1879 to 1881. In 1882 he became curate of St. Mary's,
Lewisham. The same year he took charge of the mission at
Catford, and on the formation of the parish of St. Laurence was
appointed first vicar thereof 1888. In 1891 he became rural
dean of Lewisham.

1882 | REGINALD GEORGE DUTTON.
1884 /   Son of the Hon. John Thomas Dutton, of Hinton House, Hants.
Born 20th June, 1857. Trinity College, Cambridge, B.A., 1880;
M.A., 1883. He was curate of All Saints', Lambeth, 1880 and
1881, and in 1882 came to St. Mary's. He had charge of the
Hither Green mission, which he resigned in 1884 to take up a
curacy at St. Martin's-in-the-Fields. He was afterwards preacher
assistant, St. James's, Piccadilly. While visiting a parishioner
he caught scarlet fever, from which he died 16th Nov., 1886.

MS. Notes.

Index of Names

(Persons and Places).

Subject Index

The End.

www.ingramcontent.com/pod-product-compliance
Lightning Source LLC
Chambersburg PA
CBHW032356280326
41935CB00008B/593